Work organisation and globalisation

Volume 8, Number 1, Autumn 2014

Published by Analytica Publications Ltd.
2 John Campbell Road, London N16 8JZ, UK
www.analyticapublications.co.uk
phone: +44 (0)20 7249 5931
fax: +44 (0) 7226 0813
email: orders@analyticapublications.co.uk
(for subscriptions and editorial queries)

in the UK in association with Merlin Press Ltd.
96 Monnow Street, Monmouth NP25 3EQ, UK
www.merlinpress.co.uk
phone: +44 (0)1600 775663
fax: +44 (0)1600 775663
email: orders@merlinpress.co.uk

Printed and bound in the UK by Lightningsource UK Ltd.
6 Precedent Drive
Rooksley
Milton Keynes
MK13 8PR, UK

Edited by Ursula Huws
Designed by Andrew Haig Associates

ISBN: 978 0 85036 626 6
ISSN: 1745-641X

© Analytica Publications, 2014

All right reserved. No portion of this publication may be reproduced, stored, or transmitted in any form whatsoever without the express permission of the publisher.

Cover photograph: "Starker Gezeitenstrom, Ladungsarbeiten bei schwierigen Arbeitsbedingungen" by Buonasera. Licensed under Creative Commons Attribution-Share Alike 3.0 via Wikimedia Commons - http://commons.wikimedia.org/wiki/File:Starker_Gezeitenstrom,_Ladungsarbeiten_bei_schwierigen_Arbeitsbedingungen.jpg#mediaviewer/File:Starker_Gezeitenstrom,_Ladungsarbeiten_bei_schwierigen_Arbeitsbedingungen.jpg

Labour in the circuits of global markets:
theories and realities

edited by Ursula Huws

About this journal

The globalisation of world trade in combination with the use of information and communications technologies is bringing into being a new international division of labour, not just in manufacturing industry, as in the past, but also in work involving the processing of information.

Organisational restructuring shatters the unity of the traditional workplace, both contractually and spatially, dispersing work across the globe in ever-more attenuated value chains.

A new 'cybertariat' is in the making, sharing common labour processes, but working in remote offices and call centres which may be continents apart and occupying very different cultural and economic places in local economies.

The implications of this are far-reaching, both for policy and for scholarship. The dynamics of this new global division of labour cannot be captured adequately within the framework of any single academic discipline. On the contrary they can only be understood in the light of a combination of insights from fields including political economy, the sociology of work, organisational theory, economic geography, development studies, industrial relations, comparative social policy, communications studies, technology policy and gender studies.

Work organisation, labour and globalisation aims to:

- bring together insights from all of these fields to create a single authoritative source of information on the new global division of labour, combining theoretical analysis with the results of empirical research in a way that is accessible both to the research community and to policy makers;
- provide a single home for articles which specifically address issues relating to the changing international division of labour and the restructuring of work in a global knowledge-based economy;
- bring together the results of empirical research, both qualitative and quantitative, with theoretical analyses in order to inform the development of new interdisciplinary approaches to the study of the restructuring of work, organisation and labour in a global context;
- be global in scope, with a particular emphasis on attracting contributions from developing countries as well as from Europe, North America and other developed regions;
- encourage a dialogue between university-based researchers and their counterparts in international and national government agencies, independent research institutes, trade unions and civil society as well as policy makers. Subject to the requirements of scholarly peer review, it is open to submissions from contributors working outside the academic sphere and encourages an accessible style of writing in order to facilitate this goal;
- complement, rather than compete with existing discipline-based journals
- bring to the attention of English-speaking readers relevant articles originally published in other languages.

Each issue addresses a specific theme and is also published independently as a book. The editor welcomes comments, criticisms, contributions and suggestions for future themes. For further information, visit the website: http://www.analyticapublications.co.uk.

Editorial board

Work organisation labour and globalisation is edited by **Ursula Huws,** Professor of Labour and Globalisation, University of Hertfordshire and the director of Analytica Social and Economic Research, UK. The editorial board includes:

Elmar Altvater, Department of Political and Social Sciences, Free University of Berlin, Germany
Chris Benner, Department of Community Development University of California, Davis, USA
Manuel Castells, Emeritus Professor, Department of City and Regional Planning, University of California, Berkeley, USA
Mikyung Chin, Department of Political Science, Ajou University, Korea
David Coates, Worrell Professor of Anglo-American Studies, Wake Forest University, North Carolina, USA
Sujata Gothoskar, Programme Officer, Committee for Asian Women and Researcher, International Union of Foodworkers, Mumbai, India
Jörg Flecker, Scientific Director, Forschungs- und Beratungsstelle Arbeitswelt (FORBA), Austria
Barbara Harriss-White, Professor of Development Studies, Queen Elizabeth House, Oxford University, UK
Vassil Kirov, Institute of Sociology, Bulgarian Academy of Sciences, Sofia, Bulgaria
Doreen Massey, Faculty of Social Sciences – Geography, Open University, UK
Pamela Meil, Institut für Sozialwissenschaftliche Forschung (ISF), Germany
Niels Møller, Department of Manufacturing, Engineering and Management, Technical University of Denmark
Vincent Mosco, Canada Research Chair in Communication and Society, Queens University, Canada
Rajneesh Narula, Professor of International Business Regulation, University of Reading Business School, UK
Markus Promberger, Head of Welfare, Labour and Social Inclusion Research, IAB (Institute for Employment Research), Federal Employment Agency, Germany
Norene Pupo, Director, Centre for Research on Work and Society, York University, Canada
Monique Ramioul, Head of Labour Sector, Higher Institute of Labour Studies, Catholic University of Leuven,Belgium
Keith Randle, Professor of Work and Organisation, University of Hertfordshire, UK
Gerhard Rohde, Head of Industry, Business and Information Technology Services, UNI, Switzerland
Gérard Valenduc, Research Director, Fondation Travail-Université (FTU), University of Namur, Belgium
Geert van Hootegem, Professor of Sociology, Katholieke Universiteit Leuven, Belgium
Anita Weiss, Professor of Sociology, National University of Colombia, Colombia

Visit our website: http://www.analyticapublications.co.uk

Contents

Labour in the circuits of global markets: theories and realities
Ursula Huws   1

The containment of labour in accelerated global supply chains: the case of Piraeus Port
Pavlos Hatzopoulos, Nelli Kambouri and Ursula Huws   5

Regressive safety practices in the globalised shipping industry
Suresh Bhardwaj   22

Chinese Overseas Foreign Direct Investment and the Sino-Serbian Strategic Partnership
Graham Hollinshead   37

'Sorry mate, you're finishing tonight': a historical perspective on employment flexibility in the UK film industry
Will Atkinson and Keith Randle   49

Old wine, new bottles and the Internet
Guglielmo Carchedi   69

Theories of immaterial labour: a critical reflection based on Marx
Henrique Amorim   88

Review: From Silicon Valley to Shenzen: global production and work in the IT Industry
Enda Brophy   104

Review: Flip-flop: a journey through globalization's backroads
Liz Heron   107

Visit our website: http://www.analyticapublications.co.uk

Labour in the circuits of global markets:
theories and realities

Ursula Huws

Ursula Huws is Professor of Labour and Globalisation at Hertfordshire Business School, University of Hertfordshire, UK.

ABSTRACT
This article introduces the contents of this volume, reflecting on the commonalities and complementaries between articles.

In the eight-year history of this journal, this issue was the first to be advertised, not as focused on any particular theme but as entirely open to any contribution relevant to our aims. Given the broad and interdisciplinary range of articles submitted to us, we were expecting an eclectic range of articles, covering themes normally omitted because they fall outside the scope of the selected theme. To our surprise, nothwithstanding the diversity of our authors and the vagaries of the peer review process, the articles eventually selected exhibited some very strong commonalities and complementarities, strong enough, indeed to warrant bringing them together under the joint umbrella of the title of this current volume: *Labour in the circuits of global markets: theories and realities*.

Some of these articles develop and expand on theoretical questions that have been raised in previous volumes. Others provide empirical evidence that illustrates earlier themes, deepening our understanding and raising new questions for the future.

One important recurrent theme in past volumes has been the multiple shifts and interfaces between processes involving mental labour and those involving physical labour in contemporary production and distribution processes. Conceptually, this blurring of boundaries and interdependence also makes it difficult to distinguish between the 'virtual' or 'knowledge-based economy' on the one hand and the so-called 'real' economy on the other. Some scholars insist that an immaterial or knowledge-based economy has a fundamentally different character from one based on the manufacture of physical goods and that this changed reality requires a reconception of traditional concepts such as 'labour', 'value' and 'class'. Others are equally emphatic that the two are integrally connected, forming different aspects of the same whole economy (albeit more complex than in earlier periods) and following the traditional rules of political economy.

This issue includes two important theoretical articles, by Guglielmo Carchedi and Henrique Amorim respectively, using a Marxist framework to grapple with these questions. Carchedi's focus is on how immaterial labour should be conceptualised, whilst Amorim takes issue with the concepts of 'value', 'labour' and 'class' used in recent debates about the knowledge economy. We hope that these will take the debates forward and encourage further contributions.

The empirical studies presented in this volume also illustrate the complexity of the relationship between 'head' and 'hands' in labour and production processes. Will Atkinson and Keith Randle demonstrate, in their historical study of 'below-the- line' labour in the British film industry, that the blurred and shifting line between manual labour and so-called 'creative' or 'aesthetic' labour is not a new phenomenon of the Internet Age but characterised work in the creative industries through most of the 20th Century. In their analysis of how workers 'got in and got on' in studios that were already part of a global film industry, they demonstrate that, even during a period generally characterised as 'Fordist', when trade unions were relatively strong in the industry, work trajectories were nevertheless fluid and precarious, shaped by class and gender, with a large, and often unacknowledged, role played by informal networks and educational and social capital in determining success, prefiguring many of the features of employment in present-day creative industries.

Each of the other three studies presented here provides a different window into the current global restructuring and consolidation of supply chains, increasingly under the domination of large trans-national firms, but requiring the co-operation of nation states to provide access to the necessary infrastructure. In doing so, they shine a light onto the relatively neglected role of the logistics workers through whose hands goods pass on their accelerated routes across the globe from factories to ships to ports and then by road and rail networks to the warehouses from which they are distributed to supermarkets or directly to consumers, in processes whose co-ordination, once again, requires a complex meshing of blue-collar and white-collar labour.

Graham Hollinshead, in his case study of a new bridge across the Danube in Serbia, shows the tight interconnections between political and economic motivations in the development of new infrastructure. He demonstrates that the Chinese government's Sino-Serbian Strategic Partnership and the Chinese-sponsored 'Bridge of Friendship' under construction near Belgrade are strongly linked to aspects of Chinese Overseas Foreign Direct Investment (OFDI). The bridge, located in a country whose relations with the EC are somewhat strained, and perhaps selected for that reason, opens up the prospect of a speedy road route into Europe from its eastern periphery, a route along which will flow goods manufactured in China, or by Chinese-based companies in production facilities in other countries to the east of the European Union.

This has interesting parallels with another case study, analysed by Pavlos Hatzopoulos, Nelli Kambouri and myself, of the container port at Piraeus in Greece, the largest portion of which was transferred to the Chinese shipping company, Cosco, after the 2009 sovereign debt crisis, when the Greek government was obliged to dispose of many of its assets under the stringent conditions imposed on the loans made to it by the 'Troika' (the International Monetary Fund, European Central Bank and European Commission). Under Cosco's management, the port became, in effect, a free trade zone within the European Union, acting as a trans-shipment hub between sea routes to the east and existing and newly-planned road and rail routes through the Balkans and further sea routes to the rest of Southern Europe. During this period, the productivity of Piraeus Port grew faster than any other in the world and it became the third-busiest container port in the Mediterranean, with ambitions to become the busiest. This case study does not only illustrate, like that of the Serbian bridge, the complex interconnections between public and private, local and global, economic and geo-political factors; it also investigates the impact on the labour force, caught in the squeeze between these interlocked interests, that has produced these astonishing productivity increases.

The result casts new light on another issue that has been discussed extensively in past issues of this journal (as well as in the article by Atkinson and Randle in this issue): that of the precarity of labour. Before 2009, the dockworkers in Piraeus Port were extremely well organised, with good collective agreements and working conditions that conformed to international standards. With the arrival of Cosco, the collective agreement was abandoned and most workers were re-employed via subcontractors on indeterminate, on-call contracts at reduced wages and with poor working conditions in a new regime which has been characterised as 'disciplined precarisation'. However it is questionable to what extent this extreme precarisation can be attributed simply to the requirements of a global company operating in a ruthless international competitive environment and to what extent it can be linked to the general trend of precarisation across the Greek labour market which was exacerbated as a result of the debt crisis but was already in evidence beforehand. We must conclude that precarisation is a complex and multi-faceted phenonomenon. The fragmentation of the workforce and the diversity of public and private sector actors playing a direct or indirect part in shaping these working conditions creates challenges for labour both in terms of organisation and in terms of where to direct its demands. In this particular case, the workers organised a strike whilst the article was being written, making it possible to explore these questions to some extent.

The next article takes a more extreme case of fragmentation in a globalised industry. Its focus, taking us a step back down the supply chain, is on the shipping industry, in which there are typically three key players: the ship owner; the charterer; and the ship manager, in addition to the many different sub-contractors they employ. As Suresh Bhardwaj (who has the distinction of being a Master Mariner in addition to his academic credentials) explains, because each party has a different interest, this results in a 'split-incentive' phenomenon in a common enterprise that mitigates against addressing the causes of accidents in an extremely hazardous industry. Taking advantage of the Flag of Convenience system, the industry is able to shop around among labour regimes and recruit its workforce from the poorest countries, isolating them from many of the sources of support available to other workers. Bhardwaj's main focus is on health and safety practices, which are driven by regulations which are, in turn, only introduced on the basis of evidence from accident investigations. The way these investigations are carried out, however, places the focus firmly on what happens on board the individual vessel, leading to a tendency to blame the individual worker for 'human error'. This approach renders invisible the role played by systemic practices, dictated by management imperatives taking place on-shore, either within the managing company or further up the value chain, that create the stressful conditions on board ship. This results in a paradox: while safety requires attention to how workers negotiate risks and uncertainties in everyday practice, in the contemporary shipping industry workers are increasingly denied the opportunities for socialisation, rest and organisational support that make such negotiation possible. This leads to a general downward spiral in safety practices.

The ship, the dock and the road bridge constitute just three points in the long value chains that lead from the designer's drawing board to the factory to our homes. This volume ends with reviews of two books that, in very different ways, map longer journeys taken by particular products. The first, reviewed by Enda Brophy, looks at global production and work in the IT Industry 'from Silicon Valley to Shenzen'. The second, reviewed by Liz Heron, follows the journey of the flip-flop from manufacture to final consumption.

These are welcome insights into a global division of labour on which further research, both theoretical and empirical, is urgently required.

© Ursula Huws, 2014

The containment of labour in accelerated global supply chains:
the case of Piraeus Port

Pavlos Hatzopoulos, Nelli Kambouri and Ursula Huws

Pavlos Hatzoppulos is a senior researcher in the Educational Unit at the Foundation for Research and Technology, Greece.
Nelli Kambouri is a senior researcher in the Centre for Gender Studies at Panteion University, Greece.
Ursula Huws is Professor of Labour and Globalisation at Hertfordshire Business School, University of Hertfordshire, UK.

ABSTRACT

This article presents a case study of the sale of two of the three piers at the formerly state-owned container port of Piraeus, in Greece to a Chinese company, COSCO, formng a crucial hub in the transit of goods to European markets, and examines the impacts on labour. It places this study in the context of the global consolidation, restructuring and acceleration of supply chains as well as in the specific context of privatisation of infrastructure and deregulation of labour in Greece in the aftermath of the debt crisis. Anatomising the tangled dynamics of deterritorialisation and reterritorialisation, it illustrates the complexity of the interrelationships between specific local factors and global forces in reshaping work. It also shows how the fragmentation of labour resulting from these impacts makes it easy for global corporations in the logistics sector both to consolidate their power and to evade contemporary forms of labour mobilisation. After chronicling the forms of resistance adopted by workers at the port, the article concludes by reflecting on the implications for organisation along the increasingly tightly integrated supply chains which link the labour of production workers with that of logistics workers.

Introduction

One of the most striking, but least visible, features of the Internet Age has been the speed with which the virtual and the real have been knitted together in the circuitry of global markets, using processes that compress and decompress space and time like the air inside an accordion. In doing so, they do not just consolidate control of these markets in the hands of a relatively small number of global players, they also radically restructure the relationship between the public and the private, concentrating power in supranational corporate entities away from public scrutiny or accountability. The global markets that are currently reaching maturity rest not only on global divisions of labour (geographically dispersed, though centrally managed) but also on global systems of communication and distribution. These in turn rest on infrastructures which are increasingly interconnected, both with each other and with the value chains of the commodity producers.

As the interfaces become more fluid between the ordering, manufacturing and delivery of goods and services (between production and consumption more broadly) the boundaries shift between the firms supplying these functions, and the competition between them intensifies, each encroaching on the territory of its neighbours, resulting in tectonic sectoral shifts. Manufacturers become retailers which become wholesalers which become shipping companies. Telecommunications companies morph into broadcasters which in turn gobble up publishers. Toy companies merge with software companies to produce online games featuring characters developed by movie companies. Brands (whose owners manufacture nothing directly) attach themselves to everything from shoes to clothes to bags to jewellery to perfume.

Underlying these dynamic shifts is a cold logic of consolidation in which the processes carried out online (advertising, ordering, customer service and management of the elaborated value chains by which commodities are produced and distributed and the co-ordination of all these interconnected functions) are increasingly integrated with the physical circuits of goods: the transport of materials across land and ocean from mine to refinery to factory to assembly plant to depot to warehouse to the supermarket or directly to the home of the consumer.

This creates an imperative for global corporations to maximise their access to and control of the infrastructure – whether this involves the telecommunications networks used for online communication or the physical infrastructure (and preferably both) – so that goods can reach their markets as quickly and cheaply and frictionlessly as possible.

Shifting control of infrastructure

During most of the 20th century, much of this infrastructure was owned and maintained by national governments: postal and telecommunications services, seaports, airports, roads and railways, giving national governments the power to set standards, charges and terms of use and to monitor traffic across frontiers. The first big sell-offs to the private sector, starting in the 1980s, were of telecommunications and of airports, in a process begun by the UK Thatcher Government (which privatised both British Telecom and the British Airports Authority in 1984). Telecommunications privatisation was pushed at the European level into becoming a requirement for all EU Member States, first covered in the Utilities Directive in 1990 (Directive 90/351), then (after European Commission Green papers were published in 1994 and 1995) a European telecoms market was formally brought into being on 1 January 1998, with a further 2002 Directive (Directive 2002/21) setting out a common regulatory framework for the 'electronic communications sector'. Postal services went the same way, with last EC member states abolishing the remaining sections of their national post monopolies in

2013 (Hermann, 2014) after a 15-year process of creeping privatisation (via Directives 97/67, 2002/39 and 2008/6).

Meanwhile, another series of EU Directives brought about the 'demonopolisation' of rail networks, covering, respectively cross border freight (Directive 2001/12). Track Allocation and access charges (2001/14), and access to the Trans European Rail Freight Network by licensed rail freight operators (2004/51). And, by the end of 2010, 22% of Europe's 404 main airports were either wholly investor-owned or had public-private partnerships (National Center for Policy Analysis, 2014).

What happened in Europe took place in a more piecemeal way across the rest of the world, pushed by various policies adopted by the International Telecommunications Union (founded in 1992) and the World Trade Organisation (see Huws, 2012 for a fuller discussion of these).

Many of these formerly State-owned services have become major global corporations in their own right, with over 20 featuring repeatedly among the top 100 companies listed in the UNCTAD World Investment Report from 1996 to 2006 (Clifton & Diaz-Fuentes, 2008). Increasingly, however, their sectoral identities as universal service providers are blurring as they move into other activities. Simultaneously, their traditional terrain is being aggressively targeted by companies from other sectors. Amazon, for instance, formed partnerships with US Postal Services in several US states to provide Sunday deliveries of goods to its customers in 2013 (Greenfield, 2013) under a deal whose terms were kept secret, though it was revealed that the agreement would 'not require USPS to pay employees overtime and that the scheduling needs related to Sunday delivery ... will be handled by existing staff' (Adinolfie, 2013). Since then, Amazon has also set up its own independent delivery service in California (Bensinger & Stevens, 2014). Meanwhile Google has established a rival 'Shopping Express' service in Silicon and San Francisco, with plans to expand over most of Northern California, delivering retail products straight to homes on the same day they are ordered online, in direct competition with Amazon (Wohlsen, 2014).

Restructuring and acceleration of supply chains

Amazon's strategy, sometimes described as its 'Flywheel of Growth' (see for instance Kirby & Stewart, 2007) is based on maximising the selection of products, using scale to lower the cost of goods, and accepting very small profit margins in order to do so. This logic extends beyond its role as a retailer to its role as a hardware manufacturer. Jeff Bezos, Amazon's founder, is quoted as saying that 'We sell our hardware near break-even, so we make money when people USE the device, not when they BUY the device' (Hof, 2012). This strategy depends crucially on getting the goods to customers as speedily as possible, which in turn requires tight supply chain management – 'planning and co-ordinating the materials flow from source to user as an integrated system' (Christopher, 2013:6). Amazon has also recently begun to take advantage of its monopsonistic position by aggressively putting pressure on its suppliers to reduce their prices, including using sanctions such as refusing to accept pre-orders for e-book titles from Hachette and videos from Warner Brothers, until these companies agree a price deal more favourable to Amazon (Rushe, 2014).

In Amazon's case, as with offline supermarkets such as Walmart, Tesco and Carrefour, control of this supply chain has been tipped in favour of the buyer, rather than the producer. In an apparent paradox, this control becomes tighter even as supply chains get longer, through additional levels of outsourcing. With the manufacture of very similar products increasingly dispersed, and the growing importance of the supply chain, it has been argued that we are moving into an era where competition takes place not between companies but between supply chains, a competition that is exacerbated in a context of shortening product life cycles. As Christopher (2013:12) notes: 'There are already situations arising where ... the life of a product on the market is less than the time it takes to design, procure, manufacture and distribute that same product! ... the means of achieving success in such markets is to accelerate movement through the supply chain'. The Amazon-type model, in which distribution is directly controlled by the retailer, is not, however, the only model. According to industry analysts, the majority of large companies outsource their logistics and supply chain functions to third party logistics (3PL) companies, with 86% of US Fortune 500 companies reported as doing so in 2012 (Armstrong and Associates, 2013). These 3PL companies, alongside shipping companies, rail companies, and some production companies, jostle for position with the retailers and ecommerce companies for control of their section of the supply chain, with many attempting to extend into neighbouring functions: by ousting their neighbours along the chain, by entering into strategic alliances with them, or bypassing them by using alternative routes and means. There are therefore a number of competing corporate players vying for control of logistics, but sharing the common goal of shortening the time to market as much as possible. We refer to this group collectively in this article as 'logistical capital'.

Labour in global supply chains

In this cut-throat race, what is happening to labour? Most consumers are dimly aware that the goods they have ordered online from retailers, with so little physical effort, do not just appear on their front doorsteps by magic. They may even be aware that they have been produced by means of an intricate global division of labour, involving the extraction of raw materials in one part of the world, their manufacture into products in a second and their assembly in a third (to take a rather simple example). The suicides of Foxconn workers in 2010 (China Labor Watch, 2010) brought public attention to the sweatshop conditions in which electronic goods marketed by companies like Apple, were assembled. More recently, there have also been campaigns highlighting poor conditions and low pay in Walmart, where Chinese-made goods are sold and where strikes were organised on 'Black Friday' in the USA in 2013 (Open Democracy, 2014), as well as television documentaries and articles exposing the tightly-monitored and pressurised work routines in Amazon warehouses (BBC Panorama, 2013; Head, 2014). What is less apparent is how the tasks carried out by these atomised and closely supervised workforces are interconnected and what processes guide the journey of the matter that passes so swiftly through their overworked hands.

Occasionally, against all the odds, a direct message gets through. In September 2012, Stephanie Wilson, a New York resident, bought a pair of rain boots from Saks

Fifth Avenue and found in the paper shopping bag a letter, headed 'Help! Help! Help!', written by a worker incarcerated in a Chinese prison where inmates were expected to work 13-hour daily shifts producing paper bags for up-market firms, including Saks (Greenhouse, 2014). A similar letter, also asking the finder to contact a human rights organisation, was found inside a package of Halloween decorations sold at Kmart in Oregon (Jacobs, 2013). Forced labour is an extreme example of exploitation. Workers who enter the labour market voluntarily and have acceded to the discipline of the workplace are unlikely to take such steps. For insights into their working lives we must rely on occasional journalistic accounts, reports from trade unions and NGOs seeking to improve their conditions and research carried out by social scientists. Qualitative research studies, too numerous to list here, have been carried out in a number of locations along the new global value chains, but tend, for understandable reasons linked with the difficulties of negotiating access to multiple locations, to be carried out on single sites, be they factories, warehouses or customer service call centres. In a few cases, research has been carried out in two or more adjacent links in the value chain, in order to gain an insight into the impact of restructuring on employment. Examples of these are the comparative case studies on the changing relationship between production and logistics in the food and drink and clothing industries carried out in the EC-funded WORKS[1] project (see, for instance, Huws et al, 2009; Flecker et al, 2007). These are rare windows into processes which are still poorly understood in their detail.

This article aims to add an additional window, drawing on research in progress into one transit point in global supply chains: the container port of Piraeus. This not only represents a key entry point from the east into Europe's markets; it also provides a particularly dramatic example of the impact of the privatisation of formerly public infrastructure in enabling private companies to seize control of supply routes. In this case, the company concerned is Cosco, a Chinese shipping company which was able to purchase 85% of the capacity of the container port in the 'fire-sale' of Greek public assets (Phillips, 2011) following the 2009 debt crisis.

The case study

The research which forms the basis of this article is being carried out collaboratively as part of a project led by the University of Western Sydney and funded by the Australian Research Council, from 2013 to 2016, entitled 'Logistics as global governance: labour, software and infrastructure along the New Silk Road'. Building on past research in the container ports of Shanghai, in China, Sydney, in Australia and Kolkata, in India (in the *Transit Labour*[2] project), it will investigate the container ports of Piraeus, in Greece and Valpairaiso, in Chile, as well as revisiting Kolkata and Sydney, using a collaborative Research Platform approach.

A Research Platform is seen by Kanngieser, Neilson and Rossiter (2010) as 'a research tool for transcultural mapping'. Its use in the *Transit Labour* project is described in the following terms:

---

1 See http://www.worksproject.be/
2 See http://transitlabour.asia/

This project investigates changing material and conceptual connections between labour, mobility and subjectivity in the whirlwind of Asian capitalism. Moving across three cities – Shanghai (2010), Kolkata (2011) and Sydney (2012) – it employs a platform methodology to move beyond both the activities of the monastic scholar who writes theory and the sole researcher who does fieldwork. Each city becomes the site of a research platform that combines online and offline methods to gather researchers from across the world and bring them into collaborative relation with local participants through workshops, site visits, symposia, exhibitions, mailing lists, blogs and publishing. There is an emphasis on processes of inter-referencing between the three cities. The aim is to flee the data-mined, self-referential universe of social networking sites by building a multilingual environment for collaborative invention and the common production of knowledge.

This article is based on research carried out in Greece by Helen Kambouri and Pavlos Hatzopoulos, complemented by the first two of several site visits (in November, 2013 and July, 2014) by international researchers from Australia, Canada, Chile, India, Italy, Greece and the UK as well as by desk research carried out by Ursula Huws. During the research the team met with local informants, including representatives of local workers and community organisation. This was supplemented by a series of presentations from the research team, other local researchers and stakeholders. It therefore represents work in progress. These preliminary results will be followed by others in the future.

The context

Until 2009, the Greek port of Piraeus, located 10km south of the centre of Athens, was entirely run by the Piraeus Port Authority SA (OLP), a private company that was founded by the Greek state in 1999. Currently, the Greek state owns 74% of the company's shares. In 2009, a 35-year concession agreement of part of Piraeus terminal between the Greek state, OLP and Cosco, a Chinese, state-owned shipping, logistics and port management company took effect. From then on, under the terms of this agreement, the container port was divided into two parts: Pier I continues to operate under OLP, while Pier II and, from 2013, the newly-constructed Pier III, are operated by Piraeus Container Terminal SA - PCT, a Cosco subsidiary company operating under Greek law.

The concession agreement stipulated that OLP would retain the role of the sole competitor to Cosco's business at the container port; OLP retained the right to commercially utilise Pier I of the container terminal, a space that was practically constructed from scratch between 2009 and 2011, but cannot expand further since it is adjacent to the passenger section and Pier II of the port. Moreover the concession agreement stipulated that no other container facilities shall be constructed around a 200 kilometer radius near Piraeus by any other company.

As a result of the Cosco concession, Piraeus has swiftly become a major gateway for the distribution of Chinese goods across Europe and has stimulated further interest for Chinese investments in public infrastructures that are under privatisation in the context of the austerity and structural readjustment policies adopted by the Greek governments

following the debt crisis of 2009. As Captain Fu Cheng Qiu, the CEO of PCT, states:
No other country in Europe offers such potential. We believe that Piraeus can be the biggest port in the Mediterranean and one of the most important distribution centres because it is the gateway to the Balkans and southern Europe. (Smith, 2014).

The port's growth has indeed been phenomenal in recent years. Piraeus ranks today as the third busiest container port in the Mediterranean (after Valencia and Algeciras in Spain). The port posted a 20% increase in traffic in 2013, on top of the massive 77% rise recorded in 2012 (the highest in the world). Piraeus Container Terminal (PCT), the local subsidiary of China's Cosco, handled 2.52 million twenty-foot equivalent units (TEUs) in Piraeus in 2013. When that is added to the 644,000 containers handled at Terminal I, operated by OLP, Piraeus handled a total of over 3.16 million TEUs in 2012 (Bellos, 2014).

The continuing expansion of the infrastructures within and outside the container port is expected to (and probably will) make it the busiest in the Mediterranean in the future. The new Pier III is set to expand in order to increase the port's capacity by more than 30%. A new freight centre is currently under construction in the Thriassio plain, linked with the port by an already-operational rail link. According to PCT management and the Greek government, these infrastructures will enable the port to grow still further and will result into Piraeus becoming a transit port for goods being transported via train and trucks to central and eastern Europe.

While the rise in productivity is dramatic in all piers, PCT piers enjoy a considerable advantage: 500,000 TEUs for PCT against 200,000 for OLP (Mylonas 2013). Data presented by the the Commercial Director of Cosco-PCT (Vamvakidis, 2013) also show a large increase of productivity in Pier II. The average moves per quay crane per hour according to the data presented have increased from 13.10 in 2010 to 19.45 in 2011 and 24.85 in 2012 – nearly doubling over the two year period since the granting of the concession, which comes with a port upgrade and the scaling up of other Chinese logistics interests in Greece.

The deterritorialisation and reterritorialisation of Piraeus Port

The growth of Piraeus port has been presented in Greek public discourse as one of the most - if not *the* most - important investments in the Greek economy since 2009. The Greek government has symbolically linked the Cosco concession to the expected recovery of the Greek economy and the effective management of the sovereign debt crisis through neoliberal austerity policies. On several occasions since 2009, state officials from both Greece and China have visited the PCT facilities in order to celebrate the concession as a mutually beneficial Greek-Chinese venture, bringing growth, employment and competitive advantages to both nations.

The limited research that has been conducted on the topic tends to be quite as state-centric as these government pronouncements and the dominant media reports. Most academic and policy analysis of the Cosco concession emphasises the threat that the Chinese investment in Piraeus may pose for European economies, including the threat of invasion of counterfeit Chinese goods (re)labelled 'European' after entering the Greek port (Van der Putten, 2014; Mihalakas, 2011).

This dominant state-centric discourse, however, obscures the current dynamics of de-territorialisation and re-territorialisation pursued by global capital. On the one hand, Piraeus has become a hub within the global supply chain, especially by taking advantage of its geographical position. Piraeus is the first European port after the Suez canal in the East-West container shipping lanes and has the capacity to efficiently serve through-feeder ships ports around the Black Sea, including Turkey (Vamvakidis, 2014). The post-Cosco growth of the container terminals is thus directly connected to the rise of transit and transhipment cargo (which constitute more than 75% of its total traffic) and can be counterposed to the simultaneous decreasing volume of cargo that is driven by Greek imports and exports. The increased container traffic in Piraeus since 2009 can be almost entirely attributed to the expansion in the transit and transhipment of containers, which enter the port and are unloaded and then reloaded onto other ships, trucks, trains or airplanes for different destinations without ever entering into Greek territory.

There is no customs, control or taxation implemented by the Greek state in this movement of cargo. Piraeus' development into a transhipment hub, or China's gateway to Europe, took place without engaging with the messiness of the Greek economic crisis. The Piraeus container terminal port is expanding in capacity and in business in disconnection from the Greek economic space and its surrounding areas. In spatial terms the de-territorialised nature of Piraeus' growth can be observed in the sharp contrast between the booming container port itself and the surrounding environment, mainly the Perama municipality, which remains one of the poorest areas in Greece, with rising unemployment– mainly due to the closure of the ship repair industry (Hatzopoulos & Kambouri, 2014).

On the other hand, these de-territorialising dynamics are inherently linked to new forms of re-territorialisation. PCT's presence in the Piraeus container terminal is dependent on the presence of the Greek state and the multiple arrangements that have been struck between these two institutions, both formal and informal. The port's growth is also dependent on further public or public/private investments in the modernisation of infrastructures and the creation of transport corridors that can physically link the Piraeus hub to other hubs in global supply networks. Examples of this type of infrastructural project are the construction of the Piraeus-Thriassio rail link and the planned development of a new freight centre in Thriassio. The Greek state's authority over the port is also affected by the designation of Piraeus as a space under privatisation by the Troika[3]. In this sense, the production of the space of Piraeus port is constituted by the presence of multiple authorities and regulatory arrangements. Piraeus is far from exceptional in this respect, and it is necessary to acknowledge and investigate not just its particularities but also what it has in common with other logistical hubs around the world.

Impact on labour: disciplined precarisation

Since 2009, austerity policies and rising unemployment in Greece have contributed to the imposition of a new labour regime, which has completely undermined existing labour

---

3   The term 'Troika' refers to the trio of the European Commission, European Central Bank and International Monetary Commission who together laid down stringent conditions for lending to indebted European countries after the sovereign debt crisis.

relations, amending labour law, abolishing collective agreements and damaging existing labour time and payment rules. The constant threat of unemployability has rendered new forms of precarisation commonplace especially for the younger generations, who are employed on a short-term basis with indeterminate working times, threatened constantly with imminent unemployment. The precarisation of labour in Greece since the economic crisis is no longer limited to particular sectors and groups (such as domestic work, migrant work and creative industries) but is spreading to all sectors, including those in which labour was previously disciplined and unionised.

In this context, Piraeus port has been divided into two labour worlds: the OLP side, where older dock workers with permanent contracts and guaranteed overtime are employed; and the Cosco side, where younger dock workers are employed under extremely precarious conditions. The OLP labour world has been persistently diminishing since 2009, when the Cosco concession was introduced, and has been facing a constant threat of extinction. At the end of 2012, OLP was employing 1,206 workers, mostly dockers unionised along the lines of the Dockworkers' Union – the Port of Piraeus, was a founding member of the International Dockworkers Council (IDC). Labour relations on the OLP side are primarily structured via the collective agreement signed between the unions and OLP's management, buttressed by the implementation of international labour, health and safety standards on dock work. Under the austerity programmes followed by Greek governments, OLP has not been allowed to hire any new workers, while existing workers have suffered severe wage cuts that have been applied right across the Greek public sector (Gogos, 2014). At the same time, the entire company is currently under privatisation, along with several other commercial Greek ports, both large and small. At the time of writing, the privatisation process of OLP is in its second phase, in which the six investment groups – one of them being Cosco – who have submitted their expressions of interest are preparing to table their binding offers for buying the company.

In Piraeus Port's other labour world, Cosco's subsidiary, PCT, aided by the lack of stipulations on the regulation of labour relations in the concession agreement, has opted to completely disregard the existing arrangements in Piraeus Port. These were based on a labour pool system and the existing collective agreements between OLP and the existing dock worker labour unions that were in place. According to the president of the nationwide Federation of Port Employees (OMYLE), abandoning these agreements allowed PCT instantly to reduce labour costs by around 30% in comparison with those at OLP (Georgakopoulos, 2014).

In place of the strong unionisation, fixed labour contracts, well-paid work and overtime and strictly-observed health and security standards that were in place for Piraeus dockworkers employed by OLP, in 2009, the Cosco concession signalled the institution of a new labour regime largely based on the precarisation of labour combined with practices of strict discipline of the work force. Working conditions in the PCT terminal appear increasingly to be paradigmatic of the spread of these new forms of precarisation in all the sectors of the Greek economy.

The PCT labour regime could be described for the moment more as a 'black hole' than a clear-cut hell. Little is known about working conditions and labour relations, while gaining access to PCT's facilities is extremely difficult if not impossible.

The PCT container terminal is currently the only one in Europe where workers are not unionised; workers are practically prohibited by the company from forming any sort of collective representation. In the words of one fired ex-worker in the PCT terminal:

Unions and collective bargaining are strictly forbidden...There are no 'unionising forbidden' signs but people who speak up are fired and there is an atmosphere of sheer terror. (Batsoulis, 2014).

Of the approximately 1,000 workers employed currently in the PCT terminals, only 261 were officially declared as PCT employees in 2013 (as evidenced by the 2013 PCT Annual Financial Statement)[4]. The remainder are hired through a complex web of subcontractors, orchestrated by a local logistics company, Diakinisis SA. The same ex-PCT worker described the situation in these words:

Between each employee and the company [PCT] there are two or three intermediaries. Out of one man's wages, two or three layers of contractors get their cut. (Batsoulis, 2014).

These employees have only individual job contracts, work on call, have no fixed schedules and are predominantly called to work in the piers with only a few hours notice. PCT dockworkers are generally low paid and do not get paid regular overtime. The president of OMYLE provides an illustration by referring to complaints received by his union from PCT workerswho have been given fixed 35-euro wages for shifts that might last up to 16 hours (Georgakopoulos, 2014).

Everyday working conditions in the PCT docks remain largely an unmapped terrain, apart from a few glimpses provided by former workers who have decided to denounce the company. Some of these ex-workers have testified that labour and safety conditions in the PCT piers are not regularly inspected by local or national authorities. Two workers who were fired by the subcontractor for whom they worked in the PCT pier when they attempted to form a rudimentary union describe the extremely *ad hoc* character of working conditions and working arrangements in the PCT piers:

You were receiving an SMS to be at work in three hours. Nobody knew which shift he would work the next day. As for me, for nine months, I never worked on the basis of a work schedule. There was no schedule at all. (Batsoulis, 2014)

Finally, health and safety standards that are internationally applied to dock work have not been regularly observed in the PCT piers (Gogos 2014). This is illustrated by the same ex-PCT employee:

Every day, we were putting our own lives and our colleagues' lives in danger. My machine had problems, which I detailed in writing at the end of each shift ...The next day, we'd go back to work and find out nothing had been done about it. (Batsoulis, 2014).

There are additional indications that labour accidents in the docks have remained largely unreported to local authorities, with injured workers being transferred to hospitals in private vehicles and without notification of the proper authorities.

The PCT labour regime has been regularly denounced in public discourse by anti-government political forces, both on the left and the right, in predominantly

---

4   See http://www.pct.com.gr/pct_site/attachments/article/7/PCT%20ANNUAL%20FINANCIAL%20STATEMENTS%202013%20GR.PDF

sensationalist terms. Labour conditions in Piraeus port are most often characterised using terms such as the 'Chinafication of Piraeus port', or referring to the 'Chinese labour standards' or 'medieval working conditions' that have been imposed by Cosco in Piraeus (eg, Vatikiotis, 2014; Rombolis, 2013). These critiques have stressed the exceptional character of this labour regime, which is often seen as the herald of an ongoing complete invasion of foreign capital into a ravaged country, and the full exploitation of a devastated labour force that has been made possible through the successive austerity programs implemented by the Greek government in recent years under the auspices of the Troika.

Against these critical analyses, that are often based on an openly racialised political imaginary in relation to China's positioning in global politics, it is important to resist the notion of the exceptionality of the labour regime in the PCT piers. Instead of relying on a stereotypical notion of a 'Chinese model of labour', it is necessary to contextualise the PCT labour regime in its broader context in the long-term processes related to the global restructuring of capital.

First, there is a significantly longer history of precarious forms of labour that pre-dated the Cosco concession and prefigured the recent transformations of the labour market in Greece. Since the 1980s, diverse forms of precarious work – informal, non-standard, atypical, non-declared, flexible, alternative, irregular, dependent work concealed as self-employment etc. – have appeared in Greece. More importantly, these have been the most rapidly-growing forms of labour, particularly in some sectors, such as services and agriculture. In this respect, the transformation of labour relations in Piraeus port marks the integration of dock work into a larger regime of precarity, a regime to which dock work was historically an exception, characterised by permanent or regular employment, a situation achieved after a long history of labour struggles and through the active unionisation of Greek dockworkers.

Second, the PCT labour regime must be placed in the specific historico-political context of the intensification of the Greek-European precarity regime since 2009, following the debt crisis, and the institutionalisation of precarity as the general condition of the labour regime in Greece. This intensification has been implemented in Greece through the increased involvement of the state in abolishing existing Fordist institutional arrangements and transferring most issues of regulation of the labour market to the aegis of the state. As a result, on top of massive unemployment (consistently over 20% from November 2011 onwards, and reaching 27.3% in April, 2014) labour rights that were in place before the economic crisis are now only enjoyed by workers in a few small pockets of business in the private sector of the economy (and usually, even then, through a 'voluntary decision' of the management of these businesses that is often represented in the media as philanthropy). This process is evident in how, for example, local residents that we interviewed in the neighboring municipalities of Drapetsona and Perama view workers in PCT as 'privileged' – at least in having a job at all, getting paid on time and earning salaries that are significantly above the minimum wage.

Third, the concept of precarity by itself is not sufficient to account for the particularities of the PCT labour regime. In many ways, precarity is too general a concept for analysing the prevailing labour relations and the power exercised over the labouring bodies of workers in Piraeus port. As Neilson and Rossiter have argued, precarity cannot be 'bound down to any single set of experiences, social situations, geographical sites or temporal rhythms ... Played out over diverse and at times overlapping institutional fields, the sign and experience of precarity is multiplied across competing regimes of value' (Neilson and Rossiter, 2008: 58-59). Along these lines, we should primarily stress the distinctiveness of these dockworkers' precarious experiences of precarity. The precarity regime in Piraeus is based on a complex mixture of flexibility and strict discipline.

The flexibility of the dockworkers' working hours is combined with the permanent existence of three eight-hour shifts that keep the terminal operations functioning 24/7, with workers only knowing a few hours in advance for how many shifts they will be required to work (none, half, one or more). Discipline is exercised physically. Indeed, the need to exercise physical dominance over the bodies of the workers within the container terminal often seems to take precedence over other forms of power. Instead of relying on the forms of digital surveillance that are made possible through the software applications that manage all activities and movements of bodies and goods within the terminal, PCT seems to prefer to enforce forms of direct, physical surveillance and containment of workers' bodies. There are no established breaks within or between shifts, but use is made of 'nightclub-style bouncers' to check workers' movements within the terminal and also to 'prevent chatting amongst employees' (Batsoulis, 2014). Rules of fairness give way to personal favouritism. For instance, instead of tying the wage system to the measurement and reward of workers' productivity as this is recorded and analysed by the terminal operating system, it seems that PCT's reward system is often based on the perceived degrees of loyalty that workers show towards the management and the various subcontractors.

Labour struggles in Piraeus Port

In the period prior to the Cosco concession, several strikes were organised by the main OLP trade unions, with the main purpose of stopping the concession from proceeding or at least delaying it as much as possible (Rapti, 2007). Because of these long periods of strikes, in 2005, Piraeus Port was downgraded by several publications to the category of a 'regional port' and lost most of its trans-shipment business. By the end of 2006 traffic had dwindled to 400,000-500,000 TEUs, from the 1.6 million TEUs handled in 2004 (Kousta, 2010). When the concession agreement with Cosco was signed in November 2008, a new series of strikes started, culminating in a one-month strike in 2009 during which the port was brought to a standstill. The main demand of the OLP trade unions was to render the 'colonialist' concession invalid, arguing that OLP was a profitable company, which, if managed properly through the use of the most advanced technologies, could contribute significantly to the development of the Greek economy. The strike ended when the Single-Member Piraeus Court of First Instance ruled that the strike was both unlawful and abusive and the government offered labour unions an agreement according to which the state guaranteed secure jobs and a voluntary retirement scheme for the workers employed in OLP.

Since 2009, the OLP unions have tried to approach the newly recruited dock workers and push towards the creation of a labour union in the PCT container terminal, but their attempts have in most cases been unsuccessful. In interviews, the representatives of the OLP unions stressed the lack of communication with PCT workers and expressed their lack of knowledge about the specificities of labour relations on the other side of the port. The only reliable information has come from two dock workers who were fired by PCT because they demanded better working conditions (Batsoulis 2014). The secrecy surrounding wages and contract details was allegedly stipulated as part of the individual agreements workers made with PCT or the sub-contracting companies that hired them. In 2014, a new series of strikes was called by OLP trade unions against the imminent privatisation of the company, while PCT workers seemed to remain outside these labour demands and struggles.

However, unexpectedly, on July 18, 2014, workers in the PCT container terminals organised their first ever strike, lasting for a day and a half (*Efimerida ton Sydakton*, 2014; Ekathimerini, 2014). Their main demands included: first, the signing of a collective labour agreement; second, the recognition of their employment as hard and hazardous to their health; third, an increase in daily pay rates and payment for working holidays, weekends and overtime; fourth, the abolition of 16-hour shifts and the establishment of breaks between shifts; fifth, the right to form a workers' committee to discuss labour issues; sixth, the recognition of labour accidents and the obligation to convey injured workers to hospital by ambulance rather than in private vehicles; seventh, the presence of five, rather than three, crew members in gangs; and eighth, the payment of back wages owed to them by various subcontractors.

Referring to the system of subcontracting its work force, PCT was able to deny direct responsibility for labour rights violations and delays in wage payments. Nevertheless, significant concessions were made. After the riot police arrived outside the port and the PCT management promised the strikers that PCT itself would meet their demands in the next ten days if the subcontractor who employed them was unable to do so, the strike was called off. PCT has pledged that workers who have already received training will gain recognition that their employment is hard and hazardous to health; that training will be provided for the rest of the dockworkers; that the Red Cross will be present to determine whether accidents require ambulances; that none of the strikers will be fired, and that the salaries that Diakinisis owed to its employees will be paid in full (Enet, 2014).

Future prospects for labour

Although in recent years the OLP trade unions have made concerted efforts to open channels of communication and express solidarity with the workers of the PCT container terminals, labour struggles in Piraeus port remain largely disjointed. The labour force in Piraeus has become characterised by fragmentation and hierarchy, segmented into precarious and non-precarious dockworkers. This has contributed to the prolongation of existing divisions in the port. Hierarchisation is also reflected in the different forms of labour struggle and the diverse labour demands that have emerged in the two sides of the port. The OLP labour mobilisations have primarily addressed the Greek state, demanding respect for recognised labour rights and attempting to salvage Fordist labour relations in the port, while the PCT workers' mobilisation have targeted foreign private capital, demanding basic labour rights that are no longer guaranteed for all workers in Europe.

The existing difficulties in aligning the labour struggles of Piraeus Port workers become even more acute when our analysis moves beyond the national horizon and attempts to contextualise them within processes of exploitation along the global supply chain. This exploratory case study of labour relations in Piraeus port raises some crucial broader questions about the tactics and strategies of labour struggles along global circuits of production and distribution. How can these struggles, although tied to local and national experiences and institutional arrangements, move beyond these territorial dynamics and acquire a transnational character? The commonalities characterising the imposition of new labour regimes in the rising nodes of the global supply chain across Europe have been highlighted by several recent studies (*Ta Paidia tis Galarias*, 2013 and Andrijasevic & Sacchetto, 2013). These analyses have helped us to identify common threads that link the labour relations and working conditions in production with those in logistics: for instance by comparing the working conditions in IT manufacturing industries created in central and eastern Europe by Chinese companies such as Foxconn and Chung Hong Electronics with the hardships facing workers in Piraeus Port.

New plans are now coming to fruition, to connect Piraeus Port to Kutna Hora in the Czech Republic, where some of these factories are located, via a new railway line. Such developments raise further questions regarding the possibilities of linking labour struggles across the new transport routes being opened by logistical capital and makes them even more pressing. This infrastructural project (connecting the port and the rail link) was initially conceived for the transportation of Hewlett Packard products from the port of Shenzhen in China to Kutna Hora via Piraeus. The opening of this new multimodal transport route embodies at the same time both the power and the elusiveness of logistical capital. While its elusiveness enables it to evade contemporary forms of labour mobilisation, its scale and power give it a capacity for domination (including in its relationship with the local state) that demonstrates the need for urgency in inventing transnational forms of organisation that can adapt and respond to the de-territorialising and re-territorialising mutations of logistical capital.

Conclusions

This case study raises a number of issues deserving of further investigation.

First, it illustrates very clearly the speed with which supply chains are being consolidated and restructured around the globe, the complicated negotiations between international capital and national states that takes place to put the necessary infrastructure in place and the readiness of companies to leap in to take advantage of opportunities thrown up by political circumstances. Political, economic and geographical factors all converge to shape the destiny of any particular hub in these supply chains, shaped by the intersecting interests of a range of powerful actors, many of whom are geographically remote from the site in question.

In this case, the actors directly or indirectly involved in shaping the future of Piraeus Port include, at a supranational level, the International Monetary Fund (IMF), the European Central Bank (ECB) and the European Commission (EC): the Troika whose draconian terms attached to the loans made to the Greek Government created the imperative to sell off its public assets, including the Port, and reduce the wages and employment rights of Greek public sector workers. At a national level, they include not only Greece, but also the Chinese state, with its close links to Cosco and its interest in improving access to the rest of Europe as a market for Chinese exports, as well as central and eastern Europe as a site for manufacturing for other Chinese-owned companies. Corporate interests in the development include not just Cosco itself, and its local subcontractors, but also Hewlett Packard, whose need to transport goods from China made it the first major customer for the transit route through Piraeus, as well as other international companies, China-based or not, that will use it in the future.

This complex network of intermeshed interests makes it difficult to pin the blame on any single specific actor for the consequences of these developments for dock labour in Piraeus. This points to a general challenge in the analysis of labour in global supply chains: the difficulty of disentangling the impact of historically and spatially specific impacts (such as, in this case, the catastrophic impact on the pay, conditions and job security of Greek workers resulting from the impact of the 2009 debt crisis) from those arising from global economic forces – the general impacts on labour of value chain consolidation and restructuring which may include intensification and speed-up of work, precarisation of working conditions and downward pressure on wages.

What is clear is that there is an urgent need for further research that goes beyond individual case studies (valuable though these are) to investigate the changing conditions of logistical labour right along the supply chain and, in the process, begin to identify which issues are capable of being addressed locally, and which will require intervention at a broader geographical and political level.

© Pavlos Hatzopoulos, Nelli Kambouri and Ursula Huws, 2014

REFERENCES

Adinolfie, J (2013) 'Why is Amazon (AMZN) Deal with US Postal Service Sealed?', *International Business Times*, November 11. Accessed on June 9, 2014 from: http://www.ibtimes.com/why-amazon-amzn-deal-us-postal-service-sealed-1465008.

Andrijasevic R. & D. Sacchetto (2013) 'China may be far away but Foxconn is in our doorstep', *Open Democracy*. Accessed on August 19, 2014 from: https://www.opendemocracy.net/rutvica-andrijasevic-devi-sacchetto/china-may-be-far-away-but-foxconn-is-on-our-doorstep.

Armstrong and Associates (2013) 'Eighty six percent of the Fortune 500 use 3PLs as global market', July 12. Acessed on 11 June, 2014 from: http://www.mhi.org/media/news/12685.

Batsoulis, D. (2014) Interview by the authors with fired ex-PCT employee, February 16.

BBC Panorama (2013) *The Truth behind the Click*, first shown 8.30 p.m. November 25.

Bellos, I. (2014) 'Piraeus port becomes Med's third biggest in container traffic', *Kathimerini*, January 19. Accessed on August 19, 2014 from: http://www.ekathimerini.com/4dcgi/_w_articles_wsite2_1_29/01/2014_536928.

Bensinger, G. & L. Stevens (2014) 'Amazon, in Threat to UPS, Tries its own Deliveries,' Wall Street Journal, April 24. Accessed on June 9, 2014 from: http://online.wsj.com/news/articles/SB10001424052702304788404579521522792859890.

China Labor Watch (2010) The Tragedy of the Foxconn Sweatshop. Accessed on June 7, 2014 from: http://chinalaborwatch.org/pro/proshow-98.html.

Christopher, M. (2013) *Logistics and Supply Chain Management*, Harlow: Pearson.

Clifton, J. & D. Diaz-Fuentes (2008) 'The new public service transnationals: consequences for labour', *Work Organisation, Labour & Globalisation*, 2 (2): 23-39.
Efimerida ton Sydakton (2014) 'Strike in the Cosco Paradise', July 18. Accessed on August 7, 2014 from: http://www.efsyn.gr/?p=218083.
Ekathimerini (2014) 'Union calls for strike at Cosco-controlled Dock in Piraeus'. August 18. Accessed on August 19, 2014 from: http://www.ekathimerini.com/4dcgi/_w_articles_wsite2_1_18/07/2014_541505
Enet (2014) 'Cosco: The strike pushed for a reaction'. Accessed on August 7, 2014 from: http://www.enet.gr/?i=news.el.article&id=439896.
Flecker, J., U. Holtgrewe, A.Schönauer, W. Dunkel & P. Meil (2007) *Restructuring across value chains and changes in work and employment: Case study evidence from the Clothing, Food, IT and Public Sector*, Report from the WORKS Project, Leuven: HIVA.
Georgakopoulos, G. (2014) Interview by the authors with president of OMYLE, April 3.
Gogos, G. (2014) Interview by the authors with General Secretary of OLP dockworkers Union, February 12.
Greenfield, J. (2013) 'Amazon Partners with U.S. Post Office To Deliver Packages on Sunday', *Forbes*, November 11th. Accessed on June 9th, 2014 from: http://www.forbes.com/sites/jeremygreenfield/2013/11/11/amazon-partners-with-u-s-post-office-to-deliver-packages-on-sunday/.
Greenhouse, E. (2014) 'An S.O.S in a Saks Bag', The New Yorker, June 3. Accessed on 7 June, 2014 from: http://www.newyorker.com/online/blogs/currency/2014/06/an-sos-in-a-saks-bag.html
Hatzopoulos, P. and Kambouri, N. (2014) 'The Logistical City from Above', *Logistical Worlds*. Accessed on August 19, 2014, from: http://logisticalworlds.org/?p=216.
Head, S. (2014) 'Worse than Wal-Mart: Amazon's sick brutality and secret history of ruthlessly intimidating workers', *Salon*, February 23. Accessed on June 7, 2014 from: http://www.salon.com/2014/02/23/worse_than_wal_mart_amazons_sick_brutality_and_secret_history_of_ruthlessly_intimidating_workers/.
Hermann, C. (2014) 'Deregulating and Privatizing Postal Services in Europe: The Precarisation of Employment and Working Conditions', *Global Research*, January 1.
Hodal, K., C.Kelly, F.Lawrence, C. Stuaart, T. Remy, I. Baqué & M. O'Kane (2014) 'Revealed: Asian slave labour producing prawns for supermarkets in US, UK', *Guardian Multimedia Investigation*, 10 June. Accessed on 11 June, 2014 from: http://www.theguardian.com/global-development/video/2014/jun/10/slavery-supermarket-supply-trail-prawns-video.
Hof, R. (2012) 'Jeff Bezos: How Amazon Web Services Is Just Like The Kindle Business', *Forbes*, 29 November. Accessed on June 10, 2014 from: http://www.forbes.com/sites/roberthof/2012/11/29/jeff-bezos-how-amazon-web-services-is-just-like-the-kindle-business/.
Huws, U. (2012) 'Crisis as Capitalist Opportunity: New Accumulation through Public Service Commodification, *Socialist Register*: 64-84.
Huws, U., S. Dahlmann, J. Flecker, U. Holtgrewe, A. Schonauer, M. Ramioul & K. Geurts (2009) *Value chain restructuring in Europe in a global economy*, Report from the WORKS Project, Leuven: HIVA.
Jacobs, A. (2013) 'Behind Cry for Help From China Labor Camp', New York Times. Accessed on June 7th, 2014 from: http://www.nytimes.com/2013/06/12/world/asia/man-details-risks-in-exposing-chinas-forced-labor.html?pagewanted=all&_r=0.
Kanngieser, A., B. Neilson, N. Rossiter (2010) 'What is a Research Platform?, *Transit Labour*, June 8. Accessed on June 12, 2014 from: http://transitlabour.asia/blogs/what-research-platform.
Kirby, J. & T. A. Stewart (2007) 'The Institutional Yes: and Interview with Jeff Bezos', *Harvard Business Review Magazine*, October. Accessed on June 10, 2014 from: http://hbr.org/2007/10/the-institutional-yes/ar/1.
Kousta E. (2010) 'Strikes end at Pireaus Port Authority following Concession Agreement' *European Industrial Relations Observatory on-line*. Accessed on August 18, 2014 from: http://www.eurofound.europa.eu/eiro/2009/12/articles/gr0912019i.htm
Mihalakas, I. (2011) 'Chinese "Trojan Horse" – Investing in Greece, or Invading Europe?', Accessed on August 19, 2014, from http://foreignpolicyblogs.com/2011/01/15/chinese-%E2%80%98trojan-horse%E2%80%99-investing-in-greece-or-invading-europe-part-i/.

Mylonas P. (2013) 'Container Ports: An Engine for growth' sectoral report *National Bank of Greece*. Accessed on August 18, 2014 from: https://www.nbg.gr/greek/the-group/press-office/e-spot/reports/Documents/Container_Ports_2013.pdf.

National Center for Policy Analysis (2014) *Air Transportation Privatization*, April 4. Accessed on 9 June, 2014 from: http://www.ncpa.org/sub/dpd/index.php?Article_ID=24280.

Neilson, B. & N. Rossiter (2008) 'Precarity as a Political Concept, or, Fordism as Exception', *Theory, Culture & Society*, 25 (7-8): 51-72.

Phillips, L. (2011) 'Greece unveils fire-sale of government assets', *EU Observer*, May 24. Accessed on June 12th, 2014 from: http://euobserver.com/economic/32385.

Port Technology International (2014) 'Piraeus becomes Med's third largest for container traffic', *Port Technology International*, January 31. Accessed on June 12, 2014 from: http://www.porttechnology.org/news/piraeus_becomes_meds_third_largest_for_container_traffic#.U5m5qnbLJ9s

Rapti E. (2007) 'Workers take strike action to prevent privatization of port operations', *European Industrial Relations Observatory on-line*. Accessed on 18 August, 2014 from: http://www.eurofound.europa.eu/eiro/2007/01/articles/gr0701029i.htm.

Rombolis, S (2013) 'The Chinafication of Labour?, *Ta Nea*, April 16. Accessed on June 12, 2014 from: http://www.tanea.gr/opinions/all-opinions/article/5012229/kinezopoihsh-ths-ergasias/.

Rushe, D. (2014) 'Amazon pulls Warner Bros movies from sales as trade dispute expands', *Guardian*, 11 June. Accessed on June 12th, 2014 from: http://www.theguardian.com/technology/2014/jun/11/amazon-warner-bros-price-hachette-lego-movie.

Smith, H. (2014) 'Chinese carrier Cosco is transforming Piraeus – and has eyes on Thessaloniki', *Guardian*, 19 June. Accessed on August 19th, 2014 from: http://www.theguardian.com/world/2014/jun/19/china-piraeus-greece-Cosco-thessaloniki-railways.

Ta Paidia tis Galarias (2013) 'Chinese capital goes to Greece'. Accessed on August 19th, 2014 from: http://www.gongchao.org/en/texts/2013/chinese-capital-goes-greece.

Vamvakidis, T. (2013) 'Piraeus Container Terminal S.A> - the South East Gate of Europe' presentation to *European Maritime Week Conference*, June 6. Accesssed on June 12, 2014 from: http://www.slideshare.net/jmceunipi/tassos-vamvakidispiraeus-container-terminal-sa-the-south-east-gate-of-europe.

Vamvakidis, T. (2014) Interview by the authors with PCT commercial director, January 20.

Vatikiotis, L. (2014) 'Cosco: An Anatomy of a "Successful" Privatisation' [in Greek], *Unfollow*. Accessed on July 7, 2014 from: http://unfollow.com.gr/print/magazine/3114-unfollow-18/.

Van der Putten, F. (2014) *Chinese investment in the port of Piraeus, Greece: the relevance for the EU and the Netherlands*. Clingendael Report. Accessed on August 19th, 2014 from: http://www.clingendael.nl/sites/default/files/2014%20-%20Chinese%20investment%20in%20Piraeus%20-%20Clingendael%20Report.pdf.

Wohlsen, M. (2014) 'With New Overnight Delivery, Google Confirms It Wants to Be Amazon', *Wired*, June, 3. Accessed on June 9, 2014 from: http://www.wired.com/2014/06/google-overnight-delivery-ends-any-doubt-that-its-trying-to-be-amazon/.

Wood, A. (2013) 'Walmart's Black Friday strikes: a new dawn for organised labour?', *Open Democracy*, 1 December. Accessed on June 7, 2014 from: http://www.opendemocracy.net/alex-wood/walmarts-black-friday-strikes-new-dawn-for-organised-labour.

Regressive safety practices in the globalised shipping industry

Suresh Bhardwaj

Suresh Bhardwaj (Master Mariner) is the Resident Director of the Maritime Training and Research Foundation in Chennai, India.

ABSTRACT

The highly fragmented structure of the globalised shipping industry necessitates a regulatory-driven environment for its basic administration. This is a highly safety-critical industry, but regulatory updates only take place **after** an accident has taken place, based on a retrospective analysis of incidents and accident investigations. This leads to the goal of avoiding the recurrence of past incidents (and arguably newer occurrences too) through regulatory updates of the instruments of the International Maritime Organisation (IMO). This paper highlights the limitations of such an approach and shows how existing health and safety practices in the shipping industry are inadequate to cope with work environments that are changing rapidly as a result of economic and technological pressures. Paradoxically, while safety requires attention to how workers negotiate risks and uncertainties in everyday practice, in the contemporary shipping industry workers are increasingly denied the opportunities for socialisation, rest and organisational support that make such negotiation possible. As a consequence, interpretations of accidents by 'experts' as matters of human error by the crew acquire the status of fact, further compounding the disempowered position of workers. This leads to a general downward spiral in safety practices. The paper draws on an exhaustive review of the relevant literature as well as empirical evidence obtained from interviews. It critiques the current operational definition of safety in the industry and concludes that the progress the shipping industry believes it is making, mainly, at present, through technology integration, is tardy and may even be regressive and counterproductive.

Introduction

Transportation is said to be the fourth cornerstone of globalisation, along with telecommunications, trade liberalisation and international standardisation. In transportation, it is maritime transport that dominates the sector, with an 80% share by volume (Hoffmann & Kumar, 2010; UNCTAD, 2013). The declining cost of marine transportation that facilitates the growth of world trade is increasingly achieved through efficient port operations, economies of scale achieved by increasing the size of ships and, importantly, the economic advantages resulting from globalisation. Shipping is today an integrated constituent of global supply chains, so marine transportation is constantly under pressure to contribute to the goals of cost reduction, time compression, reliability, standardisation, just-in-time delivery, information system support, flexibility, and customisation (Morash & Clinton, 1997).

However it must also be appreciated that maritime transport is a safety-critical industry and concerns for human safety and environmentally safe operations co-exist with attention to service quality that includes operational and managerial efficiency. This leads to an emphasis on indicators of service performance, increasingly enabled by technological applications for process efficiency, as well as safety. Shipping produces its service with the ship as its core constituent unit, operating in geographical isolation from management, with a handful of crew and in a high-risk environment.

While globalisation affects how most industries function, the impacts on the shipping industry are especially significant. This is because of the ease with which the owners of ships can register their assets in regulatory havens just by changing the flag the ships fly. This enables the industry to pick and choose between liberalised regulatory regimes to their economic advantage. Today ships fly flags of convenience (FOC) that enable them to benefit from a governing environment that is liberalised in its regulation, and further allow them to be crewed by seafarers of different nationalities. There are typically three key players in the shipping industry: the asset owner (ship owner); the asset user (charterer); and the asset operational manager (ship manager), in addition to the many different sub-contractors they employ. Because each party has a different interest and motivation this results in a 'split-incentive' phenomenon in a common enterprise.

This fragmentation has led to a regression to a compliance-driven culture as the means of governance for this globalised industry. The International Maritime Organization (IMO) sits at the apex of this process. However the IMO only facilitates the policy agenda. Policies are deliberated and acted upon by the constituent member Flag States and, ultimately, the few open-register flags of convenience with the largest registered tonnages influence the standards that emerge from this process. Furthermore, when it comes to the implementation of these policies by the individual flag states, compromises are made in order to attract and/or retain ship registry. The theory of regulation holds that regulatory politics are dominated by industrial lobbies that campaign for regulations that shield business profits and against those that burden the industry (Wiener, 2004). In this process, pressures to mandate advancements in safety practices are heavily weighed against the economic logic of minimising the costs and maximising the returns for each partnering entity. This results in a situation where progress is slow, incremental and very fragmented. There is no concerted effort to take collective responsibility for safety or drive improvements holistically, despite the fact that technological integration is bringing major changes. Accident and incident analysis still remains the most important tool for enabling lessons to be learned to prevent the repetition of accidents, although this is based on questionable methods for investigating and analysing accidents.

Ship management companies also take advantage of globalisation in their recruitment practices, typically engaging the services of specialist crewing agents who offer competitive services by recruiting labour from the new labour supply countries (Progoulaki & Roe, 2011). They further intensify the use of this global labour force through reduced and multicultural crewing and extended working hours, taking advantage of the weak labour rights and lower wage levels that prevail in these source countries. Such 'low road globalisation' practices, fuelled by constant economic pressures, severely undermine seafarers' capability to negotiate to minimise the risks associated with the hazardous environments in which they have to work. These 'organisational factors', typical of the industry, are overlooked as root causes of accidents and incidents that compromise seafarers' safety and, when accidents occur, it is usually the seafarers who are held directly to blame. This in turn triggers corrective actions that do not address the root causes of the problem, so that potentially unsafe practices persist and may even escalate. Thus, a downward spiral in safety practices is brought into being, perpetuated by the liberalised environment that subtracts regulation from workplaces. However this is also linked to tight, and sometimes competing, systems of regulation that drive workers ever harder, further compromising their position.

Methodology

The research strategy adopted for the study on which this paper is based was a literature review covering the maritime domain and that of other safety-critical industries, supplemented by qualitative semi-structured interviews with a purposefully-selected sample of shipping professionals. This strategy was adopted because, as Sharma (2008) points out, the literature within the maritime industry is scant and there is a lack of research on the topic. The maritime industry has not generated or retained researchers over time and, as a result, there have been few opportunities to study ship management in general or shipping services management in particular. Heuristics and rules of thumb remain the most common means of driving advances in this industry, rather than any scientific approach based on proper research (Bhardwaj, 2013).

For an exhaustive literature review a snowball strategy was adopted, achieved by following up on references in the studies that were initially retrieved. This literature was analysed by re-reading the texts, summarising and tabulating the key ideas, concepts and interpretations. The need to supplement this information with interviews was clear, both to obtain essential information and to access participants' views (Opdenakker, 2006). Face-to-face interviews were supplemented by email communication. The semi-structured interviews were informed by thematic guides and carried out in confidence (Denzin & Lincoln, 2007).

Six interviews were carried out in Chennai and Mumbai in India. Two of these interviewees (Investigator 1 & 2) were actively engaged in accident/incident investigations on behalf of insurance companies, Flag States and P&I clubs[1]. Two were shore-side managers (Shore Manager 1 & 2) of shipping companies with responsibility

---

1 A P&I Club is a mutual insurance association that provides cover for its members who are typically ship-owners and ship-operators for risks not usually covered by marine insurers, like third party liabilities, environmental pollution etc. Unlike a marine insurance company which is answerable to its share-holders, a P&I club is only responsible to its members and runs as a non-profit business.

for risk management and designated persons. The final two were shipboard staff (Seafarer 1 & 2) in the senior shipboard management functions of Master and Chief Engineer, interviewed while they were on leave. All six interviewees had extensive experience of handling ships of a variety of registrations. The rationale for this choice was to obtain a good breadth and depth of insights into this critical area of shipping operations.

The limitations of a regulatory-driven approach

In a compliance-driven culture any new regulation tends to get enacted only after there has been an accident, and shipping policy is rife which such examples; indeed, almost every new regulation can be easily linked to a major accident that caused it to be enacted. This approach is reactive and based on retrospective analysis. Whatever is not regulated is not controlled. There are thus large areas in which the logic of low-cost operation prevails, uncontrolled, with outright compromises to safety. This is an industry that in the main remains in the background, with no direct interface with the general public, except in the cruise sector. It therefore receives little public attention and is largely impervious to societal opinion and pressure. Thus shipping companies remain free to act in their own self-serving interests. The regulation-driven approach also creates a 'command and control' environment where corporate goals are met through manipulation of regulations and the regulators. This in turn generates secrecy: a 'siege mentality' sets in, in which safety issues, records and performance are not made transparent either internally or externally and no genuine lessons are learnt. Seafarer 2 comments:

The shore based management, in order to meet short term objectives of notional compliance, put excessive focus on low-frequency incidents by addressing trivial issues (like missing lifebuoy, slips, trips and burns) whilst shying away from any real safety concerns that could have serious consequences. This actually creates a false sense of safety and major issues are buried under the carpet.

This seafarer is a worker at the cutting edge of ship operations, and his comment highlights the wide chasm that exists between him and his managers on shore, who are responsible for providing him with support but who, instead of caring for his safety, seem to be driven by commercial motives.

Investigator 1 makes a similar point, saying:

Yes, the trivial matters are obvious to the naked eye of any inspector or superintendent. But the culture has to change and that can happen only when the commercial pressures become less.

Safety is not regarded as a core function, but is separated from these and treated as an additional cost. This can easily lead to a situation where the main aim becomes the protection of the company rather than the employee. It can also lead to a false sense of complacency, with a failure to recognise the damaging costs to the company, in terms of reputation and indirect consequences, in the event that an accident does occur, consequences which no claim of regulatory compliance on paper would exonerate.

The limitations of accident/incident analysis

This situation is exacerbated still further by the fact that the regulations that drive the industry are based on accident/incidence analysis techniques that lack rigour and depth. Barnett, Gatfield and Pekcan (2006) suggest that this analysis is relatively immature in the maritime world, where little scientific analysis has been undertaken to identify the trends and patterns. Even less analysis has been attempted to assess the significance and frequency of organisational factors, such as the incidence of commercial pressure, or the effects of organisational culture on the classification of causal factors as 'human errors' by operational workers. Macrae (2009) notes that accidents have traditionally been viewed as individual cognitive or behavioural issues caused merely by ignorance or carelessness. In reviewing the evidence, the same author reports that studies have consistently estimated that 80% of marine accidents are caused by human factors and laments the lack of recognition of the influence of the organisational context in shaping errors. Schroder-Hinrechs *et al.* (2012) also critically review the focus of maritime accident investigations and conclude that organisational factors do not receive sufficient attention.

This was further substantiated by the interviews:

Interviewer: *It is a common perception that people physically closest to the incident are responsible for the occurrence of the incident, which may not be true. Are the investigators aware of this fact and do they exercise due caution while conducting the investigation?*

Investigator 1: *I agree to some extent. In any accident or incident the person closest has a better view of what went wrong, though he or she might not have actually committed the mistake which led to the accident.*

Interviewer: *Who are the people that carry out accident investigation? Are they always qualified or do they have too much experience in the domain, leading to hindsight bias?*

Investigator 2: *The personnel in good survey companies who conduct investigations are qualified as Marine Casualty Investigators and they possess the required technical skills and also possess due knowledge of legalities. Experience of Casualty Investigators is gained by repeated similar cases and the final output, which is the survey report, is usually vetted in-house before it is released. If the investigator approaches each case as a new one then the possibility of hindsight bias would be eliminated.*

The International Ship-safety Management (ISM) Code mandates analysis of any reported incidents or near-misses. It encourages organisations to learn lessons by analysing the underlying causal factors in any given case so that similar incidents may be prevented in the future. Here, it follows Heinrich (1931) who theorised that the underlying causes of incidents which result in near-miss occurrences and those which unfortunately lead to more serious consequences, such as fatalities and injuries, are similar. Therefore, analysing the causes of near-miss occurrences and actual accidents have equally significant benefits. However, even at the level of incident reporting, findings reveal that such analysis is notably ineffective in the shipping context.

Research shows that the companies, in an effort to comply with the requirements, do give directions for root-cause analysis of incidents, but a closer look at the procedures directing questions for conduct of such root-cause analysis on board reveal that these questions are confined to pinning down the negligence only of the on-board staff (Bhattacharya, 2012). Key underlying concerns which made incident reporting in the industry so inadequate include weak employment practices, the absence of trade union support and lack of organisational trust. The employees' fear of losing their jobs, for example, results in considerable under-reporting and this reflects deeper social issues and organisational weaknesses in the shipping industry. This is corroborated in the 2001 annual report from the Maritime Accident Investigating Branch (MAIB) UK, which, in summarising its analysis, highlighted the reasons that seafarers routinely fail to report accidents or near misses. According to this report, a main reason is that, regardless of the nature of incidents, they fear that they will be blamed for reporting them. The report concludes that 'throughout the industry, mariners are genuinely frightened that if they were known to be reporting safety deficiencies, they would almost certainly lose their jobs' (MAIB, 2001:9).

It is widely believed in the shipping industry that 'human factors' account for 80% of the root causes of all accidents. This notion is ingrained so firmly in the industry that any challenge to the argument is dismissed as whimsical. For example a study by Baker and McCafferty (2005) who reviewed accident databases from the USA, UK, Canada, Australia and Norway, concluded that human error 'continues' to be the dominant factor in maritime accidents and drew the following conclusions: first, while the total number of accidents is declining, human error continues to be the dominant factor in 80 to 85% of maritime accidents; second, failures of situational awareness and situation assessment overwhelmingly dominate; and third, human fatigue and task omission seem closely related to failures of situational awareness. However a deeper analysis of their study shows that, whilst it includes a group of root causes classified as 'management', this refers almost entirely to on-board management factors and not to the organisational influence of the way the business is managed more broadly.

Barnett *et al.* (2006) investigated cases of collision in reduced visibility involving experienced professionals, and confirmed that organisational culture plays an important part in reinforcing the appropriate behaviour required on board. If the organisation's own shore-based management team pays only 'lip-service' to its own operating policies by failing to implement them on the vessel and, at the same time, tacitly accepts or rewards deviant behaviour (not reducing speed in restricted visibility was a matter of routine), then the individual officers on board will adopt a similar cultural attitude. Simply sending the 'offenders' to remedial training would not resolve the root cause of this type of violation. Bhattachary (2009) found that managers largely subscribe to the 'human error' theory that attributes the main cause of workplace accidents and incidents to workers behaving irrationally, wrongly applying the rules or just being unmotivated. As a result, corrective actions are directed at tackling seafarers' behaviour rather than addressing the root causes of accidents. Shore Manager 2 attests, by implication, to the futility of current practices, whereby increasing amounts of paperwork are generated that actually increase the administrative burdens of the crew on-board and hampers their ability to negotiate safety in the everyday work environment. He reflects:

Root cause identification is a complex matter which requires much more effort and study to prevent recurrence, rather than corrective action which is only temporary, by introducing more check lists etc. for the crew to follow. The identification of root cause requires more input from other stakeholders.

Investigator 2 adds:

I am not sure if the trends are being analysed by management companies but they are surely being done by P & I clubs and the same is declared in their annual reports. Mostly they show 'human failure' as the cause of most of the incidents and accidents, which is a pity.

Seafarer 1 confirms this picture, lamenting that:

The remedial action being taken by management companies is then to display safety posters on board the vessel which are produced by the P&I Clubs.

Such misdirected remedial actions, aimed at the seafarer in the name of progress, actually end up exacerbating the situation by over-burdening seafarers with mundane administrative procedures, extra paperwork and panoptic oversight from the shore management. This hinders the development of mutual trust and widens the gap between the ship-based workers and shore management. Meanwhile, the root causes continue and worsen, resulting in a progressive deterioration of the entire shipping industry environment.

How globalisation affects accident/incident investigation

Guttal (2007), among many others, has argued that globalisation is a form of capitalist expansion that integrates local and national economies into a global, unregulated market. Although economic in its structure, globalisation is equally a political phenomenon, shaped by negotiations and interactions between nation states, the institutions of transnational capital and international institutions. Its main driving forces are the institutions of global capitalism, but it also needs the firm hand of states to create enabling environments for it to take root. Globalisation is legitimated by liberal democracy, which facilitates the establishment of the neoliberal national and international policies that permit globalisation to flourish, and which, in the shipping context, allow the ship operators to hire cheap crew from various crew supplying nations. The neoliberal concept of 'freedom' is tied to the notion of 'free markets' in which people are 'free' so long as they submit to the dictates of deregulated free markets. The 'race to the bottom' hypothesis argues that, in their competition to attract mobile capital, states must converge to the lowest common denominator. In conjunction with the effect of competitiveness, this provides an ideal ground for downward harmonisation in the shipping industry, impacting all aspects of business operations that derive from the overworked, fatigued and isolated crew on board the ships (DeSombre, 2008).

Shore Manager 1 describes the impact of the additional cost pressures created by these developments on ship management:

Nowadays there are so many stakeholders and the profit margin in any venture has not changed but due to many stakeholders everyone is getting only a portion of the pie and so there is an attitude of cost cutting rather than cost optimisation.

The recruitment of cheap (and therefore inexperienced and poorly trained) crew compounds the pressures on ship management and the related health risks. Shore Manager 2 comments:

The problem of sub-standard crew and their over reliance on technology has been a source of concern. The present day crew has lost touch with the axiom 'lead, log and lookout'.

The responses from the investigators shed light on how the accident/incident investigation can be marred by the split-incentive phenomenon and the outsourcing of crewing to third parties by the ship owners, leading to a lack of transparency:

Investigator 1: *There is a problem here with the advent of the ship management company concept. If the information which the surveyor is seeking is hidden from him then the surveyor is not to be blamed.*

Investigator 2: *Unfortunately, it is normally the case with ship management companies who try to shield information as much as possible but provide it only when legal intervention comes in. So I would go to the extent to say that there has to be absolute transparency from all so that the end result can be fruitful in the interest of shipping.*

Protecting the interests of business produces a kind of myopia whereby ship managers and their crewing agents tend to hide information. This leads to a situation where there is no concerted effort, no interest and no sense of ownership by managers of the collective aims of achieving long-term and well-organised improvements. In addition, the forces of globalisation play a part in severely limiting the drive to get to the root causes of accidents/incidents.

Causes constructed rather than objectively looked for?

Error investigations can have differing objectives and purposes depending on the investigator's perspective. Sanders and Neville (1991) confirm that what is deemed to be the cause of an accident depends on the purpose of the inquiry. Thus the causes of the accident may be constructed rather than objectively sought for. This is evident from the interview with Investigator 1, who states that:

Normally the Flag State [Port State] carries out the investigation to fix responsibility into aspects leading to [the accident/incident] such as human error, navigational error and incorrect ISM procedures being followed, leading to punishment of the seafarers by either withdrawal of their Certificate of competency, or arrest.

However some accident / incident investigations are commissioned by vessel owners, management companies and, more often, by hull and machinery underwriters with a sole view to establishing the apportionment of liability towards hull and machinery damage of vessels involved in the accident / incident in question. Similar investigations are carried out to establish the final settlement of the eventual claims of the vessel owners towards hull and machinery damages.

This highlights the very limited objectives that are applied when investigations are conducted in the shipping industry. Strauch (2004) argues that the objective of an error investigation should be to avoid recurrence, or even occurrence, by identifying the antecedents to the incident and eliminating or reducing their influences in the system. However, in practice economic logic prevails. In the words of Seafarer 2:

The objective is mainly commercial for apportionment of cost through apportionment of blame.

Perhaps the most damaging restriction of all in investigations into the cause of accidents is the practice of restricting the scope of these investigations to causes that are located on board the ship itself, failing to extend the inquiry into the overarching forces of poor organisational support and on-shore managerial practices. Responsibility for this approach lies in the liability and insurance regime that covers the 'negligence of seafarers clause' in insurance policies that is admissible for insurance pay-outs. Many insurance conditions explicitly exclude the possibility of compensation for management errors. For example, one set of insurance conditions relating to 'particular average[2] damage to vessel' states:

6.2 This insurance covers loss of or damage to the subject-matter insured caused by
6.2.3 negligence of Master, officers, crew or pilots provided such loss or damage has not resulted from want of due diligence by the Assured, Owners or Managers.
(Institute Time Clauses – Hulls, 1983)

The existence of such clauses severely restricts the enquiry process, putting pressure on investigators not to search any deeper than the human error that can be detected among those on board, with an implicit requirement that no cause is attributed to onshore management, which would result in insurance benefits being forfeited.

The investigators were particularly quizzed on this aspect and Investigator 1 reflected thus:

The mandate is to establish the most probable cause leading to the accident / incident. The process generally is confined to interviews of all crew members or, as required, collection of all documents such as log books etc. The voice data recorder download is collected on a disc, electronic navigation chart screen-shots are all collected. The process of interviews may take more than a day, depending on the gravity of the accident. Every effort is made to collect all relevant data as another visit to the ship may not be possible. Then a thorough study is done of data from the voice data recorder and what is needful is extracted and then the report is drafted and then the apportionment is done.

When confronted with the same suggestion, Investigator 2, however, gave a very measured response:

Whilst I would agree with the same, I would like to comment this is not always true. We as Marine Surveyors may not mention all the observations in the survey report but the same [reporting of root causes that extend to the management on shore] is done through a personal and confidential letter addressed to the Underwriters. However, whether that information is really being used for the end purpose as envisaged in this question is not known to me.

---

2   'Particular average' refers to a partial loss caused by a peril insured against and which is not a general average loss (Marine Insurance Act 1906).

In situations involving the integration of technology, matters become even more difficult because of the unscientific integration of technology into work processes in the shipping industry. Lutzhoft and Dekker (2002) analysed one case, the grounding of the *Royal Majesty*, from the perspective of the crew, with the aim of understanding the role of automation in shaping the crews' assessments and actions. Using the 'local rationality' principle, which states that 'people do reasonable things given their knowledge, their goals, and their limited resources' they converted the search for human failures into a hunt for human sense-making, asking why the action or assessment of crew members made sense to people at that time and place, and trying to understand why they did what they did. They suggest that accidents are the result of multiple factors that may all seem necessary individually, but when combined jointly are sufficient to lead to the accident. According to these authors, focusing on a single point of failure, as was done in the official accident report on *Royal Majesty*, critically misses the typical pattern of evolution, build-up, and escalation that lies at the heart of problems related to human-automation interaction. Lutzhoft and Dekker conclude that research shows that humans are not only poor monitors of automated systems, but also tend to rely on warning systems rather than manual checks.

Shore Manager 2 makes a similar point when he comments:

Being fully qualified and competent does assist but there is a factor called 'environment' under which the individual is functioning and that sometimes clouds the decision-making process.

Seafarer 1 extends this analysis to encompass the pressures faced by over-stretched crew in modern conditions:

There is also reduction in manning to be blamed, to a larger extent, as one is left to carry out multi-tasking; and also the commercial pressures of today are far more and more complex than in yester years.

Automation is often introduced because it promises quantitative improvements: it is claimed that it will reduce human error and workload and increase efficiency. But, as demonstrated by the *Royal Majesty* accident, as well as by numerous other research results (NSTB, 1997; MCA, 2006), automation has qualitative consequences for human work and safety, and does not simply replace human work with machine work. Assigning 'human error' as the cause of accidents is found to be not only convenient from the point of view of liability and insurance but also because it allows owners and managers to ignore the catastrophic potential of some of the technology in use. This makes it possible to avoid considering the conclusion that if we cannot engineer safe systems then perhaps we should not build them.

False assumptions in incident-free scenarios

Because problems only become visible when an accident occurs, there is a general perception that just before the accident everything was perfectly normal. The belief is that in normal cases working practices are entirely orderly. This renders invisible the reality that the seafarer as an operator may be engaged in a continuous process of constructing workable alignments in situations where malfunctions and deficiencies abound. Those in charge are, in effect, making a judgement call in which failure is contained within 'acceptable' bounds. In complex systems, there are 'latent pathogens' that are normally tolerated but may be 'awakened' by a specific situation and then combine to lead to an accident. The seafaring culture of 'making everything work' is a potent ground for harbouring such latent pathogens. Thus failure is redefined and abnormality becomes the new normal. The need for the seafarer to cope with abnormalities is taken as normal and evolving practices then get built on this 'new normal' that may then become fixed in new rule-making practices. Evolving practices become formalised in operating rules which in time are further recapitulated and reified in updated formal codes of practice. It is not appreciated that the evolution of such operating practices has resulted from the practical contextual normalisation that seafarers cope with in their daily practice, and from the steady accumulation of contrived empirical experiences (Wynne, 1988).

In technology-integrated scenarios such normalisation fragments the overall social nature of technology-related practices while evolving new informal practical rules for its operation. This makes it difficult, if not impossible, to develop a holistic understanding of technology applications in their full sociological context. Technologies are evaluated in terms of their external effects or risks alone, but not by the relationships that may be intrinsic to them. As science becomes an increasingly important economic resource in industrial competition, the rush to exploit scientific knowledge in the form of commercial technologies reduces the availability of time and the possibility of social analysis in pilot phases. Thus, wider systemic problems may only become apparent during the commercial lifetime of the technologies.

Discussion

The general principle adopted in accident/incidence investigation is to find the cause, in order to provide an explanation for what happened and what went wrong and take remedial action. In particular, maritime accident investigation often adopts legalistic approaches which make it difficult to acknowledge the complexity of factors involved in an accident, factors that might be more indirect than direct. Furthermore, in the technology-integrated scenarios of today, complex socio-technical systems defy the time-honoured investigation methods and familiar ways of thinking, such as the limited way of ascribing 'resultant' outcomes through cause-effect analysis, where non-linear 'emergent' outcomes accounting may be more appropriate (Schroder-Hinrechs *et al.*, 2012). In the meantime, accident investigation is constrained by the principles of 'What you look for is what you find, and what you find is what you fix' (Hollnagel, 2008). Macrae (2009) points out that learning from past accidents presents particular challenges because the sequence of events leading to any given accident often appears unique to each specific case. The lessons drawn then become equally specific and cannot be generalised to other circumstances and situations. Havold (2000) too has suggested that to learn from past accidents we need to generalise from them, drawing systematic, and widely applicable insights into their causes, and mapping causal patterns across several layers of analysis.

One explanation for these multiple failures in the investigation process lies in the perception of safety itself that underlies them. This rests on the goal of merely sustaining accident-/incidence-free conditions and creating an environment that then satisfies itself with finding immediate or direct causes of any given incident/accident. An alternative approach involves a concept of safety that focuses on everyday work, with the aim of making things go right and facilitating performance adjustment to succeed. If this approach were to be adopted, then the effort would shift consciously from mere avoidance of things going wrong to ensuring things go right. This calls for deeper insights into latent organisational factors, man-machine interfaces and human factors engineering and requires that such issues are brought out and addressed in all stages of the design of technical procedures and of the work environment. Such is the approach adopted in other safety-critical industry environments, like the offshore oil and gas sector, as Seafarer 1 points out:

I have experienced working in the offshore oil and gas sector where safety standards are very high and I do note that shipping industry has not yet evolved to thinking that safety is not just avoidance of incidents/accidents, but making sure that everything goes right, every time. The over-riding factor is certainly commercial expediency.

This difference in understanding the concept of safety itself clouds the accident investigation process, restricting it to a process where the outcomes are severely limited. The current situation is preferred by the managers in the industry not only for this reason but also because it is less complex, less time consuming and produces more tangible and apparently more concrete outputs. Investigator 1 confirms that there are pressures to keep investigations short and simple: 'most of the times the case is closed due to pressures on fees etc.', with Investigator 2 adding that:

Also there is another factor that is more predominant: that is the marine survey companies are severely short of suitably qualified and experienced manpower and they look for tangible results in doing more surveys rather than hang on to one case itself.

It is pertinent to note here that the International Civil Aviation Organisation (ICAO, 1993) has formally adopted Reason's (1993) model of error for its Member States, to facilitate a proper understanding of human factor issues and safety in aviation. Reason's identification of the role of design and managerial factors in the generation of errors has greatly influenced the contemporary treatment of human errors. Hence, it is generally accepted that human error models and taxonomies must include the ergonomic perspective or the 'systems perspective' and the organisational perspective. The systems perspective holds that individual humans are rarely the sole cause of an accident but that individuals, machines and the work environment interact in complex relationships. The organisational perspective points to the fallibility of decision makers, supervisors and others in the organisational hierarchy in line with 'domino theory' described by Bird (1974), where human errors start with failures originating from the management's attempts to control losses within the organisation (Wiegmann & Shappell, 2003). This perspective remains lacking in the shipping industry.

It must be appreciated that there is a system at work and the seafarer is a part of the wider system, notwithstanding the globalised nature of the industry. Singling out people as the causes in accident/incident investigations will not deliver sustainable improvements. It should be recognised and appreciated that organisational factors play a significant, arguably key, role in accident causation, especially in situations where little scientific analysis has been undertaken to identify general trends and patterns.

Furthermore, while accident/incident investigation remains an important tool to drive improvements, it is not exhaustive. Fundamental rethinking is called for in the understanding of safety itself, regarding it as something beyond a mere accident-/incidence-free environment but entails developing conditions in which performance is enhanced for success.

Conclusion

The appeal of 'open registers' to ship owners lay in the globalisation of employment relations that offer low wages and lower taxes. As a result, the contractual employment of seafarers, their non-existent direct relationship with owners, mixed nationality crewing, and dysfunctional communication with managers produce a situation where no support is available for crew members. A laissez-faire approach is widespread and this has resulted in significant restructuring of the maritime labour market to the detriment of the seafarer. Labour fortunes are undermined by an ideological discourse that upholds profit as a sign of efficiency that will generate the required levels of productivity to sustain economic growth for national development. This is taking place in a context of general tendencies of erosion of labour standards, fragmentation of labour and intensification of working time (Huws, 2010) As Stiglitz (2002) asserts, economic policies that purport to separate efficiency issues from equity treat labour as a commodity and run counter to the interest of workers. 'Labour market flexibility' and 'capital market flexibility' appear as symmetrical policies but have very asymmetrical consequences – and both serve to enhance the interests of capital at the expense of the welfare of workers.

The shipping industry is characterised by a strongly safety-critical environment that demands efficient crewing and organisational support for the crew to negotiate the risks. But this has also, paradoxically, created an environment where seafarers are left over-burdened, fatigued and isolated, and where their risk negotiation skills and capabilities are seriously undermined. There is a tacit assumption that the command-and-control approach to safety regulation is the only source of accountability and administration in this globalised industry, but this is belied by the reality of poor regulation-making that is itself based on weak accident investigation analysis, lacking deeper insights into organisational or socio-technological factors. Furthermore, the perception of safety itself, as merely sustaining accident-/incidenc- free conditions, severely limits progress towards safer working conditions in the industry.

The shipping industry presents a particularly striking example of one which both actively contributes to, and benefits from, globalisation whilst also becoming a victim of circumstances. The general deterioration in its vital safety practices does not just result from the general features of a deregulated economic and organisational environment, but also from a specific system of regulation that creates social and economic conditions in an industry that values efficiency and profit over industrial safety.

© *Suresh Bhardwaj, 2014*

REFERENCES

Baker, C.C.& D.B. McCafferty (2005) 'Accident database review of human element concerns: What do the results mean for classification?' Proceedings from the conference *Human Factors in Ship Design and Operation'*, Royal Institution of Naval Architects, UK.

Barnett, M., D. Gatfield & C. Pekcan (2006) *Non-technical skills: the vital ingredient in world maritime technology?* IMarEST. Accessed on 29th June 2014 from: http://www.he-alert.org/documents/published/he00515.pdf.

Bhardwaj, S. (2013) *Challenges and potential of technology integration in modern ship management practices*, PhD Thesis, University of Plymouth, UK. Accessed on 14th June 2014 from: http://hdl.handle.net/10026.1/2840.

Bhattacharya, S. (2009) *The Impact of the ISM Code on the management of occupational health and safety in the marine industry*, PhD thesis, School of Social Sciences, Cardiff University, UK.

Bhattacharya, S. (2012) 'Sociological factors influencing the practice of incident reporting: the case of the shipping industry', *Employee Relations*, 34 (1):4-21.

Denzin, N.K. & Y.S. Lincoln (2007) *Collecting and interpreting qualitative materials*, Thousand Oaks, California, USA: Sage.

DeSombre, E. (2008) 'Globalisation, competition and convergence: Shipping and the race to the middle', *Global Governance,* (14):179-198.

Guttal, S. (2007) *Globalisation, Development in practice*, 17 (4-5):523-531.

Havold, J. I. (2000) 'Culture in maritime safety', *Maritime Policy and Management*, 27(1):79-88.

Heinrich, H.W. (1931) *Industrial Accident Prevention*, New York, NY.: McGraw Hill.

Hoffman, J. & S. Kumar (2010) 'Globalisation: the maritime nexus', C.T. Grammenos (ed) *The Handbook of Maritime Economics and Business*. London: Informa Professional.

Hollnagel, E. (2008) 'Investigation as an impediment to learning', E. Hollnagel, C.P. Nemeth & S.W.A. Dekker (eds) *Remaining sensitive to the possibility of failure, Resilience Engineering Perspectives*, vol 1, Alderton: Ashgate:259-268, .

Huws, U. (2010) 'Between a rock and a hard place: the shaping of employment in a global economy', *Work organisation, labour and globalisation*, 4(1):1-7.

ICAO (1993) *Human factors digest No. 7: investigation of human factors in accidents and incidents*. (ICAO Circular 240-AN/144) Montreal, Canada: International Civil Aviation Organization.

Institute Time Clauses – Hull. (1983) *6.0 Perils*. Accessed on 17th May 2014 from: http://www.rhlg.com/pdfs/guidetohullclaims0703.pdf

Lutzhoft, M. H. & S.W.A.Dekker (2002) 'On Your Watch: Automation on the Bridge', *Journal of Navigation*, 55(1):83-96.

MAIB (2001) *Marine Accident Investigation Branch Annual Report, 2001*. Accessed on 1st May 2014 from: www.maib.gov.uk/cms_resources/annual%20report%202001.pdf .

Macrae, C. (2009) 'Human factors at sea: common patterns of error in groundings and collisions,' *Maritime Policy and Management*, 36 (1):21-38.

MCA, (2006) MCA RP545: *Development of guidance for the mitigation of human error in automated ship borne maritime systems*, Maritime and Coastguard Agency, UK.

Morash, E.A. & S.R. Clinton (1997) 'The role of transportation capabilities in international supply chain management', *Transportation Journal*, 37 (1).

NTSB, (1997) *Grounding of the Panamanian Passenger Ship Royal Majesty on Rose and Crown Shoal near Nantucket, Massachusetts*, Marine Accident Report. National Transportation Safety Board, Washington, D.C., USA.

Opdenakker, R. (2006). 'Advantages and Disadvantages of Four Interview Techniques in Qualitative Research', *Forum: Qualitative Social Research*, 7 (4), Art. 11. Accessed on 26th April 2014 from: http://www.qualitative-research.net/index.php/fqs/article/view/175/391.

Progoulaki, M. and Roe, M. (2011) 'Dealing with multicultural human resources in a socially responsible manner: a focus on the maritime industry', *WMU Journal of Maritime Affairs*, 10: 7-23.

Reason, J. (1990) *Human error*, Cambridge & New York: Cambridge University Press.

Senders, J.W. & P.M. Neville (1991) *Human error: cause, prediction, and reduction*, New Jersey, USA: Lawrence Erlbaum Associates.

Schroder-Hinrichs, J., E. Hollnagel & M. Baldauf (2012) 'From Titanic to Costa Concordia – a century of lessons not learnt', *WMU Journal of Maritime Affairs*, 11:151-167.

Sharma, K. K. (2008) 'Integrative approach to services management: A study of global ship management', paper presented at the 10*th International Research Seminar in Service Management*, La Londe, France. Accessed on 28th June, 2014 from: http://www.cerog.org/lalondeCB/SM/2008_lalonde_seminar/Papers/S2-3-2_SHARMA_Integrative_approach_to_sces_management.pdf.

Stiglitz, J. (2002) 'Employment, social justice, and societal well-being', *International Labour Review*, 141 (1-2):9-29.

Strauch, B. (2004) *Investigating human error: incidents, accidents, and complex systems*, Aldershot, UK: Ashgate.

UNCTAD, (2013) *Review of Maritime Transport*, New York and Geneva: UNCTAD Secretariat.

Wiegmann, D.A.& S.A. Shapell (2003) *A human error approach to aviation accident analysis: The human factors analysis and classification system.* Aldershot: Ashgate Publishing.

Wiener, J.B. (2004) 'The regulation of technology and the technology of regulation', *Technology in Society*, 26:483-500.

Wynne, B. (1988) 'Unruly technology: Practical Rules, Impractical Discourses and Public Understanding', *Social Studies of Science*, 18 (1):147-167.

ACKNOWLEDGEMENTS

The author would like to thank the Maria Tsakos Foundation, International Center of Maritime Research and Tradition, Greece, for their funding contribution to the research on which this paper is based.

Chinese Overseas Foreign Direct Investment and the Sino-Serbian Strategic Partnership

Graham Hollinshead

Graham Hollinshead is Director of the Work and Employment Research Unit (WERU) at the Hertfordshire Business School, University of Hertfordshire, UK.

ABSTRACT
While considerable scholarly attention has been devoted to foreign direct investment into China, the emergent status of the People's Republic as an outward investor of growing international significance has, arguably, been subject to neglect. Yet 'going overseas' has been a fundamental element in the reform and modernisation of the Chinese economy, this policy having been formally ratified by the Chinese Communist Party in the late 1990s, with China having now ascended to the position of third most important investor abroad, after the USA and Japan. Scrutiny of the particular nature of Chinese overseas foreign direct investment (OFDI) is instructive because it reveals that, while its determinants may be familiar from a Western perspective, peculiarities are also evident, notably an integral involvement of the state in its inception. As the global spread of Chinese OFDI has now extended to Europe, this paper examines the particular case of the Sino-Serbian strategic partnership, a major element of which relates to Chinese assistance in the reconstruction of the Serbian infrastructure. This paper focuses on a Chinese-sponsored construction project on the edge of Europe. It first considers the flows and specific determinants of Chinese OFDI. The geopolitical connotations of China's economic interventions overseas are then highlighted. Finally, it offers an exposition of the Sino-Serbian strategic partnership and the Chinese-sponsored 'Bridge of Friendship' currently being constructed over the River Danube near Belgrade. The paper concludes that aspects of Chinese OFDI are powerfully conditioned by underlying geo-political and foreign policy objectives prevalent in the home country as well as economic considerations.

The flow and determinants of Chinese OFDI
According to UNCTAD statistics (UNCTAD, 2013), the flow of Chinese overseas foreign direct investment (OFDI) has risen substantially over the past three decades, standing at zero in 1981, rising to $916 million by 2000, and reaching $84 billion by 2012, rendering China the world's largest outward investor after the USA and Japan in

the early part of the current decade (Sauvant, 2013). As Davies (2012) reports, China is a late developer as an outward investor, with OFDI flows (as opposed to stocks) having grown rapidly since the Central Chinese government instigated its 'go overseas' (*Zouququ*) policy in 1999. While Asia, and particularly Hong Kong, remains the major recipient of Chinese foreign investment, there is evidence of gradual diffusion into more distant regions, including Europe, into which approximately 6% of total outward stock was directed in 2011 (Antwerp Forum, 2014). It is also apparent that, although the bulk of Chinese OFDI continues to be directed into tertiary and primary sectors (notably into leasing, manufacturing, mining, quarry and petroleum), some sectoral diversification has occurred, with 'higher' value activities, for example in the machine and electrical equipment sector, being located in Europe (Antwerp Forum, 2014; Davies, 2012).

As Nölke (2014:4) argues, the 'latecomers' of the industrialisation process 'tend towards a far more organised and coordinated version of capitalism (typically steered by banks, families, or the state) given the need to catch up with the advanced liberal economies (but to avoid colonisation)' (van der Pijl, 1998; Gerschenkron, 1962). Indeed, as multinational corporations (MNCs) from emerging market economies assume a higher global profile, considerable popular attention is being devoted to the phenomenon of 'state capitalism' (note a special report in *The Economist*, 2012). While it may be postulated that each of the BRIC[1] countries has contributed to a 're-articulation of the state-capital nexus' (Van Apeldoorn, de Graaf & Overbeej, 2012), China has been singled out for its propensity to reassert 'mercantilist' principles. While certain commentators have taken issue with the status of China as the leading global exemplar of mercantilism (note, in particular, Eswar & Wei, 2005), it is evident that the rising economic fortunes of the People's Republic have been based on a corporatist vision combining state and business interests concerning the achievement of domestic economic growth and the expression of national power (Rodrik, 2013). Accordingly, an emphasis has been placed in China upon the gearing of productive facilities towards export, as opposed to building indigenous consumer demand, with the state tending to act as 'handmaiden' to outward investors as well as the protector of domestic enterprises from adverse foreign competition (see also Rodrik, 2013).

Buckley, Cross, Tan & Liu (2007), in drawing overdue attention to the significance of indigenous institutional arrangements in determining the specific characteristics of OFDI flows, suggest that capital market 'imperfections' in China, as in other emerging economies, serve to furnish outward investing MNCs with distinctive ownership advantages. Of particular significance for the current study are two factors in evidence in China. First, state-owned enterprises may have capital made available to them at below market rates for a considerable period of time, thus creating a disequilibrium which outward-investing firms can exploit (Lardy, 1998, Scott, 2002, Warner, Hong & Xu, 2004). Second, inefficient banking systems may render soft loans available to potential outward investors, either as a product of oversight or a matter of policy (Warner, Hong & Xu., 2004; Child & Rodrigues, 2005; Ankiewicz & Whalley, 2006). In

---

1   The acronym BRIC refers collectively to the rapidly-developing economies of Brazil, Russia, India and China.

their study of the particular determinants of Chinese FDI, Buckley, Cross, Tan & Liu (2007) discover idiosyncratic as well as conventional factors at play. Accordingly, while the familiar *resource-seeking, market-seeking, strategic asset-seeking* and *efficiency-seeking* motivations postulated by Dunning (1977; 1993; 2001; Dunning & Lundun, 2008) remain valid in the Chinese context, the proximity of the state to outward investors in conjunction with the aforementioned indigenous capital market imperfections, serves to condition the form and direction of Chinese OFDI. In an intriguing departure from Western convention, Buckley, Cross, Tan & Liu (2007) reveal, in particular, that Chinese OFDI is attracted to, rather than deterred by, political risk in the target country environment, given the potential access of outward investors to disproportionate reserves of political and financial capital in their home country.

Geopolitical influences

In seeking to comprehend the distinctive features of Chinese OFDI, it is instructive to bear in mind the institutional status of China as a 'socialist market' economy, in which the state remains highly visible in many aspects of economy and society. As Yaolin Wang (2002) asserts, a 'visible hand' lies behind Chinese OFDI, with central government playing a significant role in directing its large enterprises to invest in particular regions and sectors. In accordance with the 'two resources and two markets' principle established in the early 1990s, in pursuing its internationalisation strategy, the Chinese government has 'crossed the river by feeling the stepping stones' in directing the outward investment of major enterprises over a twenty year period (Yaolin Wang:188). Yet, as China emerges as one of the leading global investors from the emerging economies, so scrutiny is growing of the motives driving this distinctive form of global capital flow originating from the East. McDermott & Huang (1996) and Zhan (1995) express little doubt that the ultimate purpose of Chinese OFDI is to further national self interest into the longer term: gaining access to foreign markets, and obtaining a stable supply of resources constitute the two overriding rationalities. Hong & Sun (2006) point to considerable complexity in the factors driving Chinese OFDI by asserting that the investment choices concerning location and sector are geared towards enhancing China's political influence within the international community and nurturing international trade relationships rather than strictly pursuing return on investment in a financially instrumental fashion.

As far as resource-seeking behaviour is concerned, and in apparent deviation from the conventional orthodoxy concerning FDI determinants, Chinese OFDI is frequently attracted to developing countries where institutional arrangements are poorly developed and political risk is considerable. A highly distinctive feature of Chinese OFDI is the undertaking of foreign construction and engineering projects accompanied by the export of Chinese manual labour to bring such projects to fruition, this policy having been endorsed by the sixth national congress of the China Communist Party (CCP) in 2002 as a major element of the prevailing overseas policy. Indeed, state-owned construction companies have enjoyed a high profile in China's drive towards internationalisation. It has been asserted (Amaghini, Rabellotti & Sanfilippo, 2011) that Chinese OFDI may be directed towards countries with an abundance of natural resources but underdeveloped institutional arrangements, a combination that creates conditions under which rents can be more easily appropriated. Moreover, while there has been no official recognition of politically-orientated FDI projects by the Chinese government, Li & Ding (1999) describe how China effectively utilised economic and diplomatic instruments to gain African support for its UN permanent membership and to mobilise against American condemnation of the Chinese human rights record in the 1970s. More recently, political leverage has been exerted on developing countries through the instrument of OFDI to further instigate international recognition of the 'one China' policy and to contain the independence of Taiwan. As Yaolin Wang (2002:189) asserts, the international 'image building', or reputational dimensions, of Chinese investment have been integral to its international spread.

According to Mbaye (2010) China is offering its experience in rapid industrialisation and poverty alleviation to the governments of developing economies as an alternative to Western-inspired modes of investment and assistance. Møller (2012) suggests that a watershed occurred in China's foreign policy, pushing it towards a novel global trajectory, as a direct result of the Tiananmen Square massacres in 1986 and the subsequent indignity the Chinese state suffered through its imposed isolation by the West. Taylor (2011) argues that China decided to put the developing world at the cornerstone of its foreign policies in order to maximise its legitimacy in these regions. In contrast to Western agencies and corporations, which have been prone to engage in institutional and governance scrutiny and critique in their transactions with the developing regions, as well as imposing economic sanctions (Taylor, 2009; Alden, 2007), China has adopted a pragmatic approach, turning a blind eye to internal issues of political legitimacy, human rights violations or corruption. The ideological empathy which has accompanied investment as it has been extended from China has been appealing to Africa in contrast with what has been perceived as Western 'apathy and scorn' (Alden, ibid; 20).

Chinese OFDI and South East Europe

The recent trend towards directing Chinese OFDI into south eastern Europe is intriguing since it retains many of the hallmarks of previous investment trajectories in developing countries, yet also manifests notable variations. Similarities include the targeting of institutionally volatile regions, the orchestration of funds flow at a bilateral governmental level, and the framing of OFDI as 'aid' through the support of projects such as infrastructure development. We should note, however, that the Sino-Serbian partnership and its associated projects are not indicative or representative of the broader pattern of Chinese OFDI into Europe. As a recent report on Euro-China investment compiled by the Antwerp Forum (2014) reveals, privately-owned enterprises have now surpassed state-owned enterprises to become major players in European mergers and acquisitions, with smaller companies proliferating in the eastern and central region in order to acquire production facilities and strategic assets. An important rationality catalysing the inflow of Chinese capital into Europe, according to the report, is to move production into export markets to circumvent (European) protectionist policies. Arguably, these developments reflect broader structural and liberalising developments in the Chinese economy through which China-based

MNCs are internationalising their assets and exhibiting market-seeking behaviours in developed and developing regions (Buckley, Cross, Tan & Liu, 2007). Reuters (2013), referring to statistics provided by the Chinese Ministry of Commerce, report that the value of all Chinese investment in Europe grew to US $77 billion in 2012, from US $59 billion in 2010, with about half the total being targeted towards 'emerging' Europe, in a region stretching from the Balkans to the Baltic states.

In the former Yugoslavia, there are close historical links with the People's Republic, China having been a stalwart supporter of the Communist regime led by Marshall Josip Broz Tito. Allegiances with individual republics continues into the post-Tito and post-socialist era. Serbia, indeed, kept its doors open to Chinese immigrants and goods during the period of international isolation imposed on it by the West in the 1990s. Prior to examining the substantive elements of the Sino-Serbian strategic partnership, it is instructive to sketch a brief historical overview of the socio-political context in Serbia. As Hollinshead and Maclean (2014) describe, in the forty years after the end of World War II, under Tito's leadership, Yugoslavia developed its own brand of 'liberal communism' associated with relative societal openness, high living standards and freedom to travel abroad for its people (Judah, 2011). The death of Tito in 1980, combined with the international collapse of communist regimes over the ensuing decade, witnessed the fragmentation of Yugoslav unity and a descent into inter-ethnic violence, accompanied by NATO bombardments and economic sanctions imposed by Western powers. In the first part of the new millennium, Serbia has found itself in a state of social and economic devastation, lagging behind neighbouring central and eastern European states which have advanced in the transition from socialism to capitalism. Hollinshead and Maclean (2014) highlight five key detrimental legacies of the 1990s. First, there was serious damage to the national infrastructure, including transport, as a result of NATO bombardments. Second, 60% of GDP was lost in the decade from 1989 to 1999. Third, around 300,000 individuals migrated to the West in the summer of 1991 at the outbreak of hostilities, including many educated people (Collin, 2001), leaving a shortage of skills. Fourth, an extra burden was placed on Serbian social services by approximately one million refugees (around 10% of the population). Finally, a deficit in educational and technological advancement was created as a result of economic sanctions and international isolation.

It may also be observed that a climate of institutional fragility persists in Serbia. A series of government coalitions over the past decade has uneasily combined reformist with retrograde party interests, the latter threatening a return to state socialism and nationalistic entrenchment. Pejovich (2004) argues that the values of collectivism and egalitarianism remain strong in the Serbian hinterland and that, among the rural, older and poorly-educated sections of the population, anti-free market sentiment remains powerful (Upchurch & Cicmil, 2004). In recent years there have been sporadic signs of growth in the Serbian economy, coupled with moves towards conciliation with the former warring states of Bosnia, Croatia and Kosovo. In October 2011, the EU offered Serbia candidate status on condition that its political relations with Kosovo were 'normalised', the former province of Serbia having gained independence.

In 2012, the nationalist politician Tomislav Nikolić unseated the pro-Western incumbent, Boris Tadić, as Prime Minister of Serbia. Nikolić's political career originated in the ultra-nationalist Serbian Radical Party, although, at the time of our research, he ostensibly supported reformist and pro-European policies, endorsing concurrently both EU membership and strong links with Russia. The economic and political prospects for Serbia remain uncertain. On a positive note, Serbia benefits from its highly skilled workforce as well as occupying a geographical hub, located between east and west, by virtue of its pivotal position in the Central Europe Free Trade Agreement (CEFTA) zone. More negatively, the fundamental institutions for market democracy have yet to be unequivocally established, with corruption, organised crime, tax evasion, financial fraud and 'crony capitalism' remaining commonplace (Gordy, 2004).

The Republic of Serbia, in common with a number of other former Yugoslav states, undoubtedly requires the injection of foreign capital in order to generate economic growth and stimulate recovery and may be classified as a 'dependent market economy' (Nölke & Vliegenthart, 2009). Given the specificities of the geo-political status of Serbia, and following the political and economic isolation imposed on it through Western measures, the receipt of investment and aid from the West is regarded with suspicion in many Serbian quarters, including government. Infrastructure development constitutes a politically sensitive field of activity from the Serbian point of view, because bridges and roads were destroyed by NATO bombardments, which also contributed to catastrophic environmental damage and high pollution levels in certain regions, notably on the Danube at Pancevo, in the vicinity of Belgrade. In the light of the continuing potency of communistic values evident within government and amongst a significant proportion of the populace at large, Serbia undoubtedly remains more receptive to financial helping hands being extended from Russia and China than from the West.

The Sino-Serbian Strategic Partnership

Friendly diplomatic relations between China and Serbia have been ongoing since October 1949, when the Federative Peoples' Republic of Yugoslavia recognised the Peoples' Republic of China as an independent state. In 2009 the accord between the countries was elevated through the inception of a 'Strategic Partnership' which promotes further cooperation in the political, economic, cultural and military fields. The bilateral agreement was signed by the presidents of the respective countries, and reaffirmed the commitment of each to the national goals of the other. Serbia, therefore, offered its endorsement of the 'one China' policy, condoning China's stance on Taiwan, while China confirmed its respect for the sovereignty and territorial integrity of Serbia, and (in contradiction to EU policy on the matter) upheld the Serbian position of opposition to the secession of Kosovo (Pavlićević, 2011).

A briefing document published by the China Policy Institute at the University of Nottingham (Pavlićević, 2011), identifies six substantive provisions within the strategic p artnership with respect to trade and industry:

First, it provides access to a free trade area of 800 million people for Chinese companies operating from Serbia by way of the free trade agreements Serbia has in force with the EU, the Central European Free Trade Agreement (CEFTA) and the

European Free Trade Association (EFTA). The possibility of entering European markets is highly desirable from a Chinese perspective, representing a prized stepping stone in its 'going abroad' policy.

Second, it commits to the construction of a 'Sino-Serbian Bridge of Friendship' over the Danube, close to Belgrade, funded mainly through a 'soft loan' from the China Exim Bank. The project is to be realised by the China Road and Bridge Company (CRBC), a state-owned concern which has enjoyed a major presence in Asia and Africa, but constitutes a new player in Europe.

Third, in the energy sector, it makes provision for the thermal power station at Kostolac to be upgraded by the China Machinery and Equipment Import and Export Corporation (CMEC). The majority of funding for this project has also been acquired through a 'soft loan' from the China Exim Bank.

Fourth, the Chinese state-owned auto manufacturer, Dongfeng, is committed to cooperating with the Serbian state-owned manufacturer FAP to produce trucks for the Serbian market, with later expansion across free trade areas anticipated. Production costs in Serbia are expected to be considerably cheaper than in other parts of Europe.

Fifth, a Serbian base is provided for the Chinese state-owned enterprise YTO, which produces tractors and farm machinery and has been manufacturing tractors in Serbia since 2010 for the local market while using a duty-free industrial zone in northern Serbia as an inventory warehouse for deliveries to markets in southern and central Europe.

Sixth, the agreeemnt consolidates the position of China's leading companies in information technology, Huawei and ZTE, which have already established a firm presence in the Serbian market (Pavlićević, 2011).

At face value, the Sino-Serbian Strategic Partnership appears to offer worthwhile benefits to both parties. From the Serbian point of view, much-needed capital inflow and infrastructural development is being offered by a 'friendly' provider on highly favourable financial terms. At a broader ideological level, the former 'pariah state' is being offered moral and political legitimacy by an emerging global superpower. From the Chinese perspective, and replicating to a considerable extent the logics underlying OFDI in developing economies, the initiative promises a highly prized entrée into lucrative European markets, sidestepping anti-dumping regulations by establishing a physical presence on the fringes of the continent. China is also seeking to build its reputation in Europe, through its apparently benign interventions in a culturally and institutionally consonant European state which ultimately stands to gain EU membership.

However, as Pavlićević (2011) asserts, both the tangible and intangible aspects of Chinese OFDI in Serbia are likely to create high dependency of the former Yugoslav state upon China, and to engender ongoing obligations for political reciprocity. Already the Serbian government has adopted a policy against joining initiatives that criticise China in international forums or condemn Chinese, or allied countries', human rights records. If Serbia is successful in securing EU membership, its complicity with China's political agenda could eventually provide a diplomatic avenue for increasing leverage by China in the domain of EU policy formulation. Furthermore, the growing physical presence of Chinese corporations on the European mainland raises the competitive stakes in Europe well above and beyond those associated with traditional exports of products from the East.

A closer look at the Sino-Serbian 'Bridge of Friendship'

In seeking to further unravel the motives for OFDI on the perimeters of Europe, we examined a 'flagship' project at ground level, namely the building of the Sino-Serbian Bridge of Friendship. Construction commenced on the Bridge in April 2011, the incumbent Serbian President, Boris Tadic, describing the project as 'a new model of infrastructure development in Serbia' (Website of the Democratic Party of Serbia, 2011). The construction is designed to span around 1600 metres, with 21.5 km. of access roads being laid, and will bridge the river Danube between the towns of Zemun and Borca close to Belgrade. A major objective of the project is to relieve traffic congestion in and around the city and to facilitate vehicular access to international trunk routes. The contractor for the project is the China Road and Bridge Corporation (CRBC) which is a large-scale, state-owned foreign trade and economic co-operation enterprise, previously engaged in infrastructure development projects in Asia, Africa, the Middle East and South America.

In its company handbook for the Serbia branch, the company states: 'Standing at the new starting point, CRBC aims at building itself into a world-class construction company of competitive edge with pioneering spirit, and incessant innovation and shaping a harmonious and win-win future with friends from all walks of life'. The total cost of the production is €170m., of which €145.5 m. is provided by the China Exim Bank, to be repaid by the Serbian government over a 15-year period at a 3% interest rate. The workforce responsible for Bridge construction is recruited from China and housed in dormitories on the construction site, permitting highly flexible shift working aiming at a speedy completion of the project.

In its publicity documentation CRBC stresses the symbolic significance and environmental friendliness of the bridge, using a logo featuring a rainbow to represent the friendship and concord between the two nations that are party to the accord, as well as sending a powerful message to the people of Serbia that the infrastructural and ecological atrocities suffered at the hands of NATO in the past are now subject to economic and moral rectification through the provision of Chinese investment and aid.

Discussion

The Sino-Serbian Bridge of Friendship may be regarded as an exceptional manifestation of international investment and aid on the edges of the continent of Europe. While infrastructural projects funded by foreign investment and orchestrated by bilateral governmental accords have been commonplace in developing economies, seldom have such developments been witnessed in a European sovereign state. Indeed a visit to the site of the bridge construction in the rural outskirts of Belgrade brings home to the observer the peculiar symbolism of the project in which an almost hermetically-sealed 'little China' work site has been transposed to these distant post-socialist soils. While the government and people of Serbia may offer a cautious welcome to their former communist ally, which is offering much needed assistance in the rebuilding of the country's infrastructure funded by a 'soft loan', there are clearly also grounds for consternation and scepticism. The investment carries with it profound geopolitical implications both at Serbian, and EU levels. For Serbia, the aid emanating from the east has been offered on a typically pragmatic basis, paying little regard to endemic and continuing levels of corruption in many walks of business and institutional life. It may be argued, however, that the succour offered by China to Serbian policy makers is misplaced, given the need for the post-socialist state to engage in a thoroughgoing institutional 'clear out' if it is to make real political and economic progress (Upchurch, M. & Marinkovic, 2013). Indeed, perhaps paradoxically, a degree of mistrust in local agencies and structures in Serbia is apparent in the investment episode itself: the Chinese contractor has shown little interest in sourcing services from local suppliers or workers, thereby limiting possibilities for broader capacity building or real vertical integration to stimulate the local economy. From an EU perspective, the growing visibility of Chinese capital on the outskirts of Europe, and in a candidate country, is likely to create concerns. The increasing dependency of the Serbian Government on China may ultimately lead to rifts within Europe on matters such as the condemnation of human rights abuses as well as delicate territorial and sovereignty issues. More generally, and in the light of the capital source disequilibria which furnish Chinese outward investors with disproportionate ownership advantages, it has been asserted (Dobson, 2014) that Chinese state-owned enterprises operating in 'western' territories, present local interests in the advanced economies with a number of complex challenges, in particular concerning safety, the environment, labour laws, transparency and national security.

Turning to the motives underlying Chinese OFDI in Europe, it may be inferred that the quest for new and larger markets is an important priority in driving Chinese mercantile intervention into Europe. In a parallel case to the Sino-Serbian Bridge Project, in the neighbouring state of Bosnia, the Dongfeng Electric Corporation has been contracted to build a hydro-electric power plant at Stanari on highly favourable terms compared to potentially competing European investors. According to a report by Reuters (2013), Chinese firms are prepared to take on risks and offer discounts in exchange for access to central and south-eastern Europe, the Balkans and neighbouring regions offering economic growth, looser regulation than the European heartlands and a place at the portals of the European Union. As the Chinese economy begins to liberalise, so its indigenous producers and consumers are seeking to ascend the international value chain and, through a type of 'reverse Marco Polo' effect (Antwerp Forum, 2014), to reap the knowledge-based benefits of direct exposure to the production of high quality goods and services in Europe. It may therefore not be too far-fetched to speculate that the bridge is not only designed to upgrade the Serbian transport infrastructure for the benefit of domestic users, but that it will also serve to facilitate the growth of an emerging hub of Chinese business interests in its south east European locality.

Undoubtedly, as the stepping stones initiated at the commencement of China's 'going overseas' policy over two decades ago begin to extend into the European region, Chinese corporations are learning, in an incremental fashion, about the realities of doing business in a comparatively highly-regulated trading bloc. The knowledge-seeking motivetherefore constitutes a fundamental driver for spawning Chinese operations in Europe, as companies may learn from the periphery prior to migrating their business further into the advanced heartlands of the continent. This study of the motives guiding Chinese OFDI also draws attention to the potent effect of political path dependency as well as institutional and cultural consonance in shaping the patterns and flows of overseas investment. As stated above, the investment flowing from China is highly conditioned by internal Chinese political considerations which have tended to favour developing and now post-socialist European regions as targets. The broader geo-political ramifications of this phenomenon can scarcely be underestimated at a time when anti-American and anti-Western sentiment is rife amongst the underprivileged majority of the world's population, and the ethical behaviours of MNCs originating from the advanced economies are being increasingly scrutinised and subject to negative campaigning.

Conclusion

Recent departures in the study of the dynamics of outward investment from the BRIC countries, including China, have effectively identified the extent to which prevalent institutional arrangements in the home environment, and particularly the role of the state, impact the behaviours of outward-bound MNCs. In contemplating the current state of play concerning Chinese OFDI into Europe a complex picture emerges. The Bridge of Friendship project in Serbia is reminiscent of an early stage of China's 'going overseas' policy, in which state-owned enterprises were key players, and an emphasis tended to be placed upon infrastructure and primary sector developments in institutionally-consonant developing economies. As the Chinese economy increasingly liberalises, and key indigenous actors seek to ascend the international value chain, so Europe, and particularly the central and eastern region, is becoming a magnet for knowledge-seeking smaller and medium-sized enterprises. Regarding such developments in their totality, it may be envisaged that China will become more visible in the continent of Europe in the future, with hubs of interconnected Chinese business life becoming more widespread.

© Graham Hollinshead, 2014

REFERENCES

Alden, C. (2007) *China in Africa* , London: Zed Books.
Amaghini, A., R. Rabellotti, R. & M. Sanfilippo (2011) 'China's outward FDI: An Industry – level Analysis of Host Country Determinants', unpublished paper presented at the CESifo Venice Summer Institute *China and the Global Economy Post Crisis* conference (18-18th July).
Antkiewicz, A. & J. Whalley (2006) 'Recent Chinese buyout activities and the implications for global architecture', Working Paper 12072, Cambridge MA: *National Bureau of Economic Research* (NBER).
Antwerp Forum (2014) *The Euro- China Investment Report 2013/2014*, Antwerp: Autonomous Management School, University of Antwerp.
Buckley, P., J. Clegg, A.R. Cross, X.Liu, H. Voss & P. Zheng (2007) 'The determinants of Chinese outward foreign investment', *Journal of International Business Studies,* 38:499-518.
Child, J & S.B. Rodrigues (2002) 'The internationalization of Chinese firms: a case for theoretical extension?' *Management and Organization Review*, 1 (3):381-410.

Collin, M. (2001) *This is Serbia Calling: Rock'n' roll radio and Belgrade's underground resistance*, London: Serpent's Tail.

Davies, K. (2012) 'Outward FDI from China and its policy context', *Columbia FDI Profiles: Country profiles of inward and outward foreign direct investment*, the Vale Columbia Centre on Sustainable International Investment.

Democratic Party of Serbia Website (2011) *Most prijateljstva- novi model infrastrukturninradiva in Srbiji*. Accessed on 24th April 2014 from: http//www.ds.org.rs/index.php?option=com content&vie w=article&id=9574:2010-07-14-16-22-17&catid=16&Itemid=431.

Deng, P. (2003) 'Foreign direct investment by transnationals from emerging economies, the case of China', *Journal of Leadership and Organizational Studies*, 10 (2):113-124.

Dobson, W. (2014) 'China's state-Owned Enterprises and Canada's FDI Policy', *SPP Research Paper no- 7-10*. Working Paper No. 2416422, *Rotman School of Management*.

Dunning, J.H. (1977) 'Trade, Location of Economic Activity And the MNE: A Search for an Eclectic Approach', B.Ohlin, P.O. Hesselbom & P.M. Wijkmon (eds.) *The International Location of Economic Activity*, London: Macmillan:395-418.

Dunning, J.H. (1993) *Multinational Enterprises and the Global Economy*, Wokingham, Addison-Wesley.

Dunning, J.H. (2001) 'The eclectic (OLI) paradigm of international production: past, present and future', *International Journal of the Economics of Business*, 8(2):173-190.

Dunning, J.H.& S.M. Lundan (2008) *Multinational Enterprises and the Global Economy*, Cheltenham: Edward Elgar, second edition.

The Economist (2012) 'The Visible Hand', special report by Wooldridge, A., *Economist*, January 21st

Gerschenkron, A. (1962) *Economic backwardness in historical perspective; a book of essays*, Cambridge, MA: Belknap Press of Harvard University Press.

Gordy, E. (2004) 'Serbia after Djindić: War crimes, organized crime and trust in institutions', *Problems of Postcommunism*, 51:10-17.

Hollinshead, G. & M. Maclean (2013) 'Reaching Distant Parts; The Internationalization of Brewing and local organizational embeddedness', J. Gammelgaard & C. Doerrenbaecher (eds.) *The Global Brewing Industry: Markets, Strategies and Rivalries*, Cheltenham: Edward Elgar:79-106.

Hong, E. & L. Sun (2006) 'Dynamics of Internationalization and Outward Investment: Chinese Corporations' Strategies', *The China Quarterly*, 187:610-634.

Judah, T. (2011) *Yugoslavia: 1918- 2003*, London: BBC History.

Lardy, N.R. (1998) *China's Unfinished Economic Revolution*, Washington DC: Bookings Institution.

Lawrence, S.V. (2002) 'Going Global', *Far Eastern Economic Review*, 165 (12):32.

Li, L. & X. Ding (1999) 'Target Selection Strategy for China's Overseas Direct Investment', *Contemporary Economics Research*, 101:46-63.

Mbaye, S. (2010) 'Matching China's Activities with Africa's Needs', A, Harriet- Sievers, S.Marks & S,Naidu (eds.) *Chinese and African Perspectives on China in Africa*, Oxford: Pambazuka:1-15.

McDermott, M. & C.H.Huang (1996) 'Industrial state Owned Multinationals from China' *Asia-Pacific Business Review*, 3 (1)1-15.

Møller, K. (2012) 'The role Kenya's civil society can play in ensuring mutually beneficial Sino-Kenya engagement', *POLIS Journal*, 7:242-282.

Nölke, A. (ed) *Multinational Corporations from Emerging Markets*, London: Palgrave MacMillan.

Nölke, A. & A. Vliegenthart (2009) 'Enlarging the varieties of Capitalism; The emergence of Dependent Market Economies in East Central Europe', *World Politics*, 61 (4):670- 702.

Onjala, J. (2008) 'A Scoping Study on China-Africa Economic Relations: The Case of Kenya'. Institute for Development Studies. Accessed on 20th April 2014 from: http://www.aercafrica.org/documents/china_africa_relations/Kenya.pdf.

Pavlićević, D. (2011) 'The Sino-Serbian Strategic Partnership in a Sino-EU Relationship Context', *Briefing Series*, China Policy Institute, University of Nottingham:68.

Pejovich, S. (2004) 'The uneven results of institutional change in Central and Eastern Europe: The role of culture', *Justice and Global Politics*, October 21-24.

Prasad, E. & J-S Wei (2005) 'The Chinese Approach to Capital Inflows: Patterns and Possible Explanations', *NBER Working Paper No. 11306*, NBER.

Reuters (2013) 'Chinese firms invest in emerging markets energy for EU toehold', *Top News*, June 11th. Accessed on 24th April 2014 from: http//www.mobile.reuters.com/article/idUSL5N0EN1CF20130611?irpc=932.
Rodrik, D. (2013) 'The New Mercantilist Challenge', *Social Europe*. Accessed on 24th April from http://www.social-europe.eu/2013/01/ the-new-mercantilist-challenge/.
Sauvant, K.P. (2013) 'Three challenges for China's outward FDI policy', *Columbia FDI Perspectives*, Perspectives on topical foreign direct investment by the Vale Columbia Centre on Sustainable International Investment, 106.
Scott, W.R. (2002) 'The Changing World of Chinese Enterprises: An Institutional Perspective', A.S. Tsui & C.M. Lau (eds) *Management of Enterprises in the People's Republic of China*, Boston: Kluwer Academic Press:59-78.
Taylor, I. (2011) *The forum on China-Africa Cooperation* (FOCAC), Oxford: Routledge.
Taylor I. (2009) *China's New Role in Africa*, London: Lynne Rienner Publishers.
Taylor, R. (2002) 'Globalization strategies of Chinese companies: current developments and future prospects', *Asian Business and Management*, 1 (2):209-225.
UNCTAD (2013) *FDI/TNC database*. Accessed on 20th April from: http://stats.unctad.org/fri/.
Upchurch, M. & S. Cicmil (2004) 'The political economy of management knowledge transfer: Some insights from experience in Serbia and Montenegro', *South East Europe Review*, 7:101- 120.
Upchurch, M. & D. Marinkovic (2013) *Workers and Revolution in Serbia: From Tito to Milosevic and beyond*, Manchester: Manchester University Press.
Van Apeldoorn, B., N. de Graaf & H. Overbeek (2012) (eds) 'The rebound of the capitalist state: the re-articulation of the state-capital nexus in the global crisis', special issue, *Globalizations*, 9 (4).
Van de Pijl, K. (1998) *Transnational Classes and International Relations*, London: Routledge.
Warner, M., N.S. Hong. & X. Xu (2004) 'Late development experience and the evolution of transnational firms in the People's Republic of China', *Asia Pacific Business Review*, 10 (3-4):324-345.
Yaolin Wang. M. (2002) 'The Motivations behind China's government initiated Industrial Investments Overseas', Pacific *Affairs*, 75 (2):187-206.
Young, N. (2012) 'You can't stay aloof forever; The political economy of Chinese investment in Africa', *The East African*, 13th February.
Zhan J. (1995) 'Transnationalization of Outward Investment: The Case of Chinese Firms', *Transnational Corporations*, 3 (4):67-100.
Zhang, Y. (2003) *China's Emerging Global Businesses: Political Economy and Institutional Investigations*, Basingstoke: Palgrave Macmillan.

'Sorry mate, you're finishing tonight': a historical perspective on employment flexibility in the UK film industry

Will Atkinson and Keith Randle

Will Atkinson is a lecturer at Hertfordshire Business School, UK.

Keith Randle is Professor of Work and Organisation at the University of Hertfordshire, UK.

ABSTRACT
This article considers the nature of employment in the UK Film Industry in the period 1927-1947 against a background of US domination of the global market for film. Drawing on archived interview material from 60 participants in the archive of the History Project of BECTU (the British trade union for Media and Entertainment workers) the article focusses on entry routes, working hours, training and pay grades to assess the degree of stability present in the labour market across a number of selected below-the-line film production occupations. This provides an historical context to debates surrounding the organisation of work in the sector, which is characterised by both continuity and change. The article argues that the UK film industry has never been a stable, 'job-for-life' sector, nor have its labour processes ever followed mass production lines. It supports assertions that assumptions of linear development from secure to casualised employment are inadequate for understanding work in this sector.

Introduction
This article considers the history of labour market flexibility in the UK film industry since the emergence of a studio system in 1927. This can be divided into three main phases: first, a transitional period of growth, interspersed with labour/capital conflict and with a fragmented internal labour market from 1927 to 1947; second, a pact between labour and capital and sector-level institutional agreements from 1948 to1990; and third, deregulation and weakening of labour organisation from 1990 onwards[1]. Little research has been published on the history of employment in the UK film industry, due in part to a shortage of empirical data on employment practices (Blair, Grey & Randle 2001:170). Literature on the UK studio system has tended to

---

1   The 1990 Peacock report encouraged greater production independence in TV, following the widening of competition for Channel 4 contracts and the series of Employment Acts between1982 and 1990.

focus on state intervention and the impact of US distribution companies in the global and domestic markets (Low, 1985; Street, 1997; Blair & Rainnie, 2000). Reflecting a trend in wider studies of work (see, for example, Hauptmeier & Vidal, 2014) there has been a lack of research bringing together a synthesis between political economy, the employment relationship and the actual experiences of film production workers. This article examines the first of the three phases above, from 1927 to 1947, against more contemporary accounts, combining a comparative political economy of the UK and US studio systems (Blair & Rainnie 2000; Wakso, 2003) with oral history testimonies of film workers employed in the UK during the 1930s.

By the 1920s film was a globalised market, dominated by US products. In response to this situation, governments worldwide introduced state regulations to defend their national industries from penetration by the USA (Guback 1969). In 1927 the Quota Act was passed in the UK. Designed to protect the national film industry, the Act also led to some important developments in the organisation of film work. In 1947 the three main film unions, the ETU, ACT(T) and NAT(K)E[2] formalised their joint control of the internal labour market through a series of agreements with employers[3].

This article examines the period before this capital-labour pact, which led to a period of relative stability and security in film employment. A comparison between this period and more contemporary accounts of the employment relationship (Blair, Grey & Randle, 2001) enables us to draw the conclusion that employment trends in the industry may have been more circular than linear, and that continuities are as prevalent as change.

The next section considers the sparse accounts of labour in the film sector, highlighting an even greater shortage of research on below-the-line and female employment in the UK film industry. A third section provides a brief account of employment flexibility in the sector today, the historical development of the UK film studios and the internal labour market. The fourth section describes the methodology underpinning the research presented here, while the fifth section presents empirical data on the nature of employment in UK film production from 1927-1947, based on archived interviews. A final section draws some conclusions.

The division of labour in film production

The costs of film production are generally divided into two categories: above-the-line (ATL) and below-the-line (BTL). This accounting device emerged in the Hollywood studio system in the 1940s and has been broadly replicated across international film

---

2   Electrical Trades Union (ETU). Association of Cine-Technicians (ACT). Formed in 1933 and became Association of Cinematograph, Television and allied Technicians (ACTT) in 1956 recognising television workers. National Association of Theatrical and Kine Employees (NATKE). Added Kine in 1936 to incorporate film production workers. The three unions merged to form Broadcasting Entertainment Cinematograph and Theatre Union (BECTU) in 1991.

3   The unions took considerable control over pay rates and labour supply with three agreements in particular: when they formalised the closed shop with the major studios in 1947; when the ACT(T) agreed minimum crewing levels with the British Film Producers Association; and when the three main unions (ACT(T) NAT(K)E and ETU) signed the demarcation agreements which formalised collective agreements over minimum pay and grades. However labour conditions improved from 1937 due to a number of studio agreements, the fair pay clause in the 1938 Quota Act and the commencement of an informal closed shop from 1941.

production ever since (Dawson & Holmes, 2012). This distinction has become, 'the most important hierarchical division between "creative" and "technical" labor' (Stahl, 2009:58). The main creative 'talent' – principal actors, directors, screen-writers and producers – are ATL and are generally considered to be the creators of the content and meaning of films (Powdermaker, 1950), while technical employees, such as camera operators, focus pullers, carpenters and boom operators, are BTL and considered to have less creative input to film content (Banks, 2010). Much of the literature focuses on ATL labour, although an increasing number of contemporary studies have taken a more inclusive approach in both the USA and the UK (Blair, 2000; Randle & Culkin, 2009; Caldwell, 2008; Mayer, 2011). The published history of BTL employment is sparse, but two contending accounts of the US sector are the most comprehensive. The first is influenced by the notion that flexible specialisation and 'vertical disintegration' have been a catalyst for transformation in the sector (Christopherson & Storper, 1987, 1989; Jones, 1996), while the second takes a political economy perspective and places more emphasis on continuity and change (Nielson, 1983; Wakso 2003). These debates are discussed in more detail later. Reid's (2008) work on the UK industry, beginning in 1950, provides an analysis of industrial relations and the labour market among ACT technicians. In the US studio system the execution/conception distinction was characterised by a strict shooting script which both determined content and controlled BTL labour with instructions from the scenario departments in pre-production and well-planned set designs from the art department (Staiger, 1985; Christopherson & Storper, 1987; 1989). In the UK, studio departments were generally under-funded and disorganised, especially in the 1930s, with scripts often completed or rewritten during production (Low, 1985; Chanan, 1976). Set building in the 1930s, from design to execution could be haphazard, last minute and created with a minimal budget.

The 'line' was reflected in the US studio system in the unions, with the Directors Guild of America (DGA) representing ATL members and the International Association of Theatrical and Stage Employees (IATSE) representing BTL members (Wakso, 2003). The three main unions representing behind-camera workers in the UK were divided by departments and trades, with NATKE and the ETU mainly representing members from general trades: carpenters, hairdressers, plasters and electricians. ACT, which represented specialised trades (boom operators, focus pullers, directors etc) included both BTL and ATL workers.

In spite of the mixture of ATL and BTL members in ACT, thje available evidence suggests that the 'line', was broadly similar in both the USA and the UK and is a useful indicator of hierarchy. However, this convenient dichotomy obscures the heterogeneous nature of BTL film labour. Hierarchy is central to organisation in the industry, with heads of department (HODs), and other managers (see Table 2) mediating control and consent in the employment relationship and recruitment in the labour market. A five-grade system is adopted here which also incorporates four occupational types in BTL employment.

The film labour process depends upon 'teamed production' (Ryan, 1991). Nevertheless, BTL occupations remain largely overlooked. ATL work has formed the focus of much greater interest, being branded as 'artistic labour', which is 'high status, and is valorised as the primary source of creativity, '"genius" and aesthetic value…' (Banks, 2010: 305). There are a number of exceptions to this, which, in examinations of the UK industry, have followed an industrial relations and/or labour process theory approach (Chanan, 1976; Jones, 1987; Ryan, 1991; Blair, 2001; Reid, 2008).

Table 1: Occupational grade in film production 1951

Occupational grade	Trades
Grade 1 - 'Creative Professionals'	Director, producer, screen writer, art director (production designer) and head lighting cameraman (cinematographer) on feature films
Grade 2 - Managers and Technical Professions	Chief hairdresser, make-up artist and costume designer, production manager, first assistant director, draughtsman, model maker, studio construction manager, gaffer (head of lighting), editors, sound mixer and camera operator (also second unit lighting cameraman)
Grade 3 - Technicians and Craft workers	Focus puller, boom operator, continuity girl (script supervisor), carpenter, rigger, plasterer
Grade 4 – Administration and assistants	Hair, make-up and costume design assistant, production secretary, third assistant director
Grade 5 – Trainees	Clapper boy, tea boy, office boy, number boy (essentially production runners)

Source: Census (1951): ORDER XXI – PERSONS PROFESSIONALLY ENGAGED IN ENTERTAINMENTS AND SPORT, Classifications of Occupations (England and Wales) HMSO.

Employment flexibility in film production: A US/UK historical comparison

Employment in contemporary UK film production

The UK film production sector has been described as a cottage industry, in which films are often produced by small companies or using individual producers who raise capital to fund a single film (Blair, Grey & Randle, 2001). Empirically-grounded contemporary literature delineates the following picture. Employment is almost universally freelance (Creative Skillset, 2014). Entry into the sector is often dependent on personal contacts followed by a period of internship which frequently involves working for free (Randle, Leung & Kurian, 2008, Percival & Hesmondhalgh, 2014). Developing a career requires building a reputation, working long hours on projects and coping with periods without paid work, sometimes with a second job outside the industry (Blair, Grey & Randle, 2001). Below-the-line workers often access employment through 'semi-permanent work groups', which are assembled by heads of department (HODs), to overcome employment uncertainty (Blair, 2001). In a deregulated labour market, informal networks and contacts are the main ways to access work (Lee, 2011;

Grugulis & Stoyanova, 2012). Employment contracts are generally 'all-in deals' (Blair, Grey & Randle, 2001:182) for the duration of a single film, often with no overtime pay or compensation for unsociable hours. Accessing and funding training is often the responsibility of the employee rather than the employer (Grugulis & Stoyanova, 2009). The division of labour is noticeably gendered, with more women in hairdressing, make-up and wardrobe departments and in the production office and a strong domination of men in lighting, studio construction, sound and camera. There is also a gender pay gap, with women on proportionally lower pay than men and often in positions lower down departmental hierarchies (Sargent-Disc, 2011).

A comparative political economy of the US and UK studio systems

The term 'studio system' stems from classical-era Hollywood[4] spanning a period from approximately 1920 to 1950 and refers to the vertical integration of the eight large Hollywood majors[5]. The majors controlled the production, distribution and exhibition of film (Christopherson & Storper, 1989). The domestic exhibition market in the USA was large enough to enable the majors to recover the cost of their investment in production. Expansion brought about the domination of the European market, which by the late 1920s provided them with their profit margins. This dominance was particularly overwhelming in the UK: in 1926, 90% of films exhibited in British cinemas were produced by the Hollywood majors (Blair & Rainnie, 2000). Influenced by theories of 'flexible specialisation' (Piore & Sabel, 1984) some have argued that in the US film sector the studio system resulted in the adoption of 'Fordist' production practices (Christopherson & Storper, 1986; 1989; Jones, 1987) in which below-the-line work was the domain of male workers with a craft identity (Christopherson & Storper, 1989), who could expect stable employment, with a 'traditional career' in 'traditional hierarchies' (Jones, 1996:58). Starting from this premise, the argument then followed that a shift towards flexible employment from the 1950s was prompted by the vertical disintegration of the Hollywood majors following the 1948 Paramount Supreme Court decision (which ended the majors' monopoly over the exhibition market) and the growth of television. This, it was contended, also led to an increase in independent production and a more flexible labour market (Christopherson & Storper, 1986, 1989). Both the extent of this 'Fordist past' and the subsequent move to flexible employment, have been challenged (Aksoy & Robins, 1992; Blair & Rainnie, 2000; Wakso, 2003; Dawson, 2012). The nature of film production, where every film is different, means that comparisons with mass production labour processes can be misleading (Dawson, 2012), while the assertion that BTL studio workers were all in stable employment at one studio is also debateable (Neilson, 1983; Dawson, 2012). In the USA, IATSE did represent all BTL crafts, but these were divided into autonomous branches that were protective of their individual trades, some of which also developed their own professional organisations (Wakso, 2003), reflecting the heterogeneous nature of film production labour and putting into question the extent to which it could

---

4   Classical-era Hollywood is often referred to in relation to the Hollywood formula picture, with studio locations and sets, in contrast to the 'New Hollywood' of the 60s and 70s with location shooting and independent production, but it also refers to the vertically integrated studio system.

5   Fox, RKO, MGM, Warner Brothers, Paramount, Universal, United Artists, Columbia Pictures

be characterised as flexible specialisation. However the suggestion that a vertically integrated studio system resulted in greater levels of employment security has wider acceptance (Scott, 2002).

It has also been suggested that emphasising the shift towards independent production, due to vertical disintegration, neglects the role distribution companies play in the circulation of capital in film. Hence, although the 1948 Supreme Court decision may have reduced the number of cinemas owned by the majors, they retained their powerful distribution arms which still dominated the domestic and global film market and, importantly, still provided the financial backing for film production. The monopoly of the world film market by the US majors has therefore continued since the 1920s (Aksoy & Robins, 1992; Wakso, 2003).

The concept of flexible specialisation was part of a wider trend towards 'paradigm break theories' in the mid-1980s (Smith & Thompson, 2010:14) that proclaimed a magic-bullet answer to the impact of globalisation across industries in developed societies. There is a need to understand the global film market as part of a larger narrative of 'horizontal integration' (Blair & Rainnie, 2000:91) with US film majors diversifying into, and merging with, other media and electrical engineering companies, and engaging in runaway production across Europe from the 1920s onwards (Wakso, 2003). It would be more accurate to see them as 'distribution companies with a small amount of production attached' (Blair & Rainnie, 2000:193). As such these distribution companies (especially MGM, Fox, and Columbia) invested in UK production (and wider European production) throughout the history of this industry (Guback, 1969).

Research in the UK (Blair & Rainnie, 2000; Blair, Grey & Randle, 2001; Blair, Culkin & Randle, 2003; Reid, 2008) has highlighted contemporary employment differences between the UK and the USA but has lacked empirical data relating to actual working lives during the UK studio system, which makes it difficult to compare past and present work experiences. There is, however a range of literature on the structure of the British studio system (Low, 1985; Wood, 1986; Murphy, 1996; Street, 1997; Blair & Rainnie, 2000), and some industrial relations literature focusing on the 1930s (Chanan, 1976; Jones, 1987), which provides data on employment in the UK from 1927 to 1947. The 1927 Quota Act stipulated that 25% of films exhibited in UK cinemas must be produced by UK studios, with a quota of 75% of UK nationals working on each production (Street, 1997). To gain a more rounded view of film history there is a need to 'merge dispassionate analysis of structures with the real life stories of those most affected by the workings of the industry' (Nielson, 1983:48). What follows is an account of the impact the 1927 Act on BTL workers in the UK during the 1930s. The aim is to build on the political economy of film and provide a synthesis with workers' accounts of employment in this period.

The Act gave UK companies some guarantee of a return on their investment and led to the vertical integration of two British majors; the Associated British Picture Corporation (ABPC), and the Gaumont British Picture Corporation (GBPC), bought by the Rank Organisation in 1941[6]. Like the Hollywood majors, these conglomerates

---

6   ABPC employed 6,000 workers in production, distribution and exhibition; it owned the ABC cinema circuit. GBPC employed 14,000 and owned the Gaumont cinema circuit. The Rank Organisation bought GBPC in 1941 and became the dominant film combine in Britain with over 600 Odeon and Gaumont cinemas (Jones 1987:61)

integrated a number of production studios, distribution companies and large cinema circuits, with interests in every stage of film from pre-production to exhibition.

Employment in British film studios rose from 4,418 to 6,638 following the Act, with approximately one third of those employed being women (Jones, 1987), the majority of whom worked in offices and female-dominated trades in production. Most employment was concentrated in 25 studios around London and the south east of England, with many more built during the 1930s[7] and many of the distribution companies located in Wardour Street, Soho, in Central London (Wood, 1986).

It is important not to overstate the growth in production or to suggest that vertical integration resulted in a London-wide studio system comparable in size and scope to Hollywood. The UK industry did not have a domestic market of a size which could provide a return on its investment; this was still mainly controlled by the eight Hollywood majors with distribution deals controlled by the powerful Kinematograph Renters Society. During the peak of UK production in the mid-1930s, 60% of films exhibited in UK cinemas were produced in Hollywood (Low, 1985). Despite state intervention in the UK, US dominance resulted in a highly volatile domestic market and created a 'feast and famine industry' (Reid, 2008), with a series of boom and bust periods from 1927 to 1947.

In the UK a two tier structure emerged. The first tier comprised the vertically-integrated studios owned by GBPC, ABPC and Rank and other in-house production companies[8], including studios owned by the Hollywood majors. In these larger studios formal departmental bureaucracies emerged, with job tenure for a number of employees, enabling unions to organise labour more easily (Jones, 1987). In the second tier were small independent companies, which rented studio space and often hired workers on a freelance basis. These companies often only stayed in business for a short period and produced low-budget 'quota quickies' for the US distributors, so they could fulfil their quota of UK productions and avoid having their bigger-budget Hollywood productions banned from its cinemas (Blair & Rainnie, 2000). Unions found it much more difficult to organise employees working for these small, sub-contracted companies (Chanan, 1976; Jones, 1987). This industrial structure suggests that a dual labour market, (Doeringer & Piore, 1971) existed in this period. However a simple distinction between 'core' workers able to gain secure employment on big budget feature films and 'peripheral' workers on insecure contracts working on quota quickies is complicated by a number of factors which are explored through the data.

There is no clear agreement on when the British studio system officially ended. ABPC 'disintegrated' in 1969 and Rank in 1979 (Threadgall, 1994). However centralised in-house production across the sector had gradually declined from the early 1950s onwards, leading some to suggest that it ended in the 1950s (Ellis, 1982; Reid, 2008). By this time many studio departments were made up of freelance workers hired for the duration of one film or TV series. Most of the studios were known as 'four-wallers', employing a small number of staff (mainly in studio construction and production

---

7   Pinewood Studios, Denham Studios and Shepperton Studios were all built in the 1930s. For a full list of studios built in this period see Wood, L. British Films 1927-1939 (BFI website at: http://www.bfi.org.uk/)

8   For instance Associated Talking Pictures (Ealing Studios), British and Dominions (Elstree, Imperial Studios) and London Films (Denham Studios)

lighting) on permanent contracts but having no in-house production (Reid, 2008). Since the 1970s there has been very little permanent employment in UK film production, with all of the studios having become 'four-wallers'.

If vertical disintegration is questionable as the catalyst for dramatic shifts in work organisation in the Hollywood context, it simply cannot be applied in the UK, where the history of film production is one of structural weakness (Blair, Grey & Randle, 2001) even during this period when in-house production dominated. The move to almost universal freelance contracts has been described as an 'extreme case of existing trends towards '"flexible" labour markets' (2001:173) rather than an early example of an industrial transformation from Fordist to post-Fordist production principles. In the US context, by contrast, this has prompted much debate (Christopherson & Storper, 1986; 1989; Aksoy & Robins, 1992; Jones, 1996; Blair & Rainnie, 2000; Dawson, 2012). Employment in the UK sector is best understood against a background both of the gradual and uneven decline of the studio structure and of the changing nature of labour organisation, to which we now turn.

Labour organisation in the UK: 1927-1990

The development of in-house production and employment following the Quota Act, led to the growth of the three main film unions during the 1930s. However at this time they were unable to gain control of the labour supply or negotiate national collective agreements with employers (Jones, 1987). Labour organisation in the ETU and NATKE strengthened throughout the 1930s, but among technicians in the ACT it did not begin to strengthen until after 1939. In 1941 the UK Ministry of Labour awarded film technicians in sound and camera 'reserve occupation' status, acknowledging their potential contribution to the war effort. To achieve this status, technicians had to first join the ACT. This increased union membership dramatically and led ultimately to the formalisation of the closed shop[9] after 1945 (Reid, 2008). From 1947-1990 the three main film unions controlled labour supply with a pre-entry closed shop, collective agreements over pay and tighter demarcation of tasks (Reid, 2008).

Employers were now obliged to recruit available freelance workers with union membership, proven via a 'union ticket', and shown to the shop steward on entering the studios. Getting a ticket was difficult; for example, approval of the application of an employer's preferred non-union candidate by the trade union panel could take a year or more (Kelly, 1966). Many interviewees who began work in the 1930s mention recommending their children and other relatives for union membership in the post-war period. Ticket holders were not guaranteed employment, but they benefited from union control of labour supply and, from the 1950s, there were increasing numbers of employment opportunities in commercial television production, to which union members had privileged access (Reid, 2008). The Employment Acts (1982-1990) ended the closed shop and national collective agreements came to an end in 1988, weakening labour organisation (Mckinlay, 2009) and resulting in an increased level of

---

9   The pre-entry closed shop was a system used by many unions across industries in the UK up until 1989, until it was made illegal by the 1990 Employment Act. Under this system, potential employees without union membership were barred from working until they had obtained membership.

employment casualisation in both film and TV production (Sparks, 1994; McKinlay, 2009).

Methodology

During the 1980s a group of film-makers keen to record the working experiences of (mainly retired) colleagues in the industry initiated the BECTU[10] History Project (BHP)[11], which resulted in an archive of over 650 interviews. Drawing on this archive, this article focuses on the production stage of film making and occupational categories in below-the-line film production work: craft workers, designers, the production office and technicians. Sixty interviews from the archive were analysed, of which all but five were with people directly involved in production departments (sound, camera, art departments, studio construction and production lighting). The remaining five interviews were with people who provide general information on employment (a production accountant, a studio manager and full-time trade union officials).

The selection method involved taking a sample of trades and grades from each production department. The interviews were conducted by more than 20 interviewers and covered themes relating to employment, film-making and film aesthetics. They are semi-structured oral history interviews, adopting a life-story approach, providing background on parental occupation, education and prior work history. All the interviewees were trade union members (as were the interviewers) and around one third were shop-stewards. Of the 55 production workers, all started in BTL positions with 19 ending their careers in high positions as 'creative professionals', a term used to describe high grade film production workers (see Mayer, 2011) in ATL and high BTL positions, 22 finishing in management and 'technical professions', while 14 ended their working lives as skilled technicians or craft workers. Twenty one were educated in elementary schools and 34 in grammar and private schools. Fifteen were women, mainly working in hairdressing, wardrobe, secretarial work and continuity, although three moved into production office or above-the-line positions. The craft and design workers migrated from general trades originally developed outside the film industry, but adapted to the specialised requirements of film production. Production office workers and technicians were in specialised trades particular to the film industry. This is an important distinction in a volatile labour market, since craft workers and designers had transferable skills which could be more easily adapted to outside industries, while specialised workers found this more difficult.

ATL employees form the majority of the 650 interviews in the archive, with accounts from BTL workers in occupations such as boom operator, continuity girl or focus puller much rarer than those from producers, for example. In particular, former NATKE and ETU members are poorly represented, with only six studio construction

---

10 BECTU (The Broadcasting, Entertainment, Cinematograph and Theatre Union) was formed in 1991 as the result of the merger of a number of different media trade unions, including the Association of Broadcasting Staff (representing BBC employees), NATTKE (National Association of Theatrical, Television and Kine Employees) the ACTT (Association of Cinematograph Television and allied Technicians) and the FAA (Film Artistes Association).

11 www.bectu.org.uk/advice-resources/history-project

workers and five former ETU members (who were employed in production lighting) in the sample.

A more general limitation of using an oral history archive is that the interviewers did not necessarily share the aims of this research or focus on employment issues. There are, for instance, interjections and redirecting questions in the interviews which sometimes move the interviewee away from relevant employment issues. Several techniques were used to sift through the interviews to discover the more relevant material. These included mapping careers using a 'data sorting' method commonly used in qualitative secondary analysis (Heaton, 2004), in which relevant data from the BHP interviews was coded to analyse workers' experiences of 'getting in and getting on'. These examined the way the workers were recruited and the ways they progressed, descriptions of the labour process, training and the nature of work. In the interviews there are recurring themes relating to the labour market, hidden in what the film production researcher Caldwell (2008) refers to as 'trade stories'. Some of these recurring accounts, for example one recurring story, here labelled, 'my Hitch story', explicitly refers to the need to build a reputation in an insecure labour market, by having worked with a 'big player' (Wakso, 2003) in the industry. The following section presents the findings from the interviews. Actual names are used because the data are not anonymised in the archive.

Working below the line: 1927-1947

The rise of HODs and BTL hierarchies

Studios were generally run by a studio manager or a central producer with a small team of unit producers, script/scenario editors, film editors and directors on long-term contracts. In the next grades down were the heads of the various departments (HODs). Table 2 provides a comparison of some of the top grades in 'entertainments and sports professions' in the occupational classifications from the censuses of 1931 and 1951. The table reveals how HOD roles emerged between 1931 and 1951, associated with the growth of in-house studio bureaucracies following the 1927 Quota Act. The emergence of these job titles is indicative of the rise of management roles in the film industry in the 1930s. Many of these top grades, which were well established in the UK by 1951, still exist today (Creative Skillset, 2014) and now recruit BTL workers further down the line into semi-permanent work groups, thereby playing a central role in the management of the labour process (Blair, 2000). Five grades in film production employment, which had emerged by 1951, have been identified here.[12] These operate across the four occupational categories (crafts, technicians, production office and designers). Each of the positions in Table 1 was held by some of the 55 interviewees at various points in their careers and all progressed to the top three grades. The positions from Grade 2 down are all considered 'below-the-line', while Grade 1 positions are generally considered 'above-the-line'. Literature on the US studio system implies that

---

12   These grades are based on several budget sheets, reflecting weekly pay rates from films produced in the 1940s and 1950s at the Fairbanks production company and in the 1960s from ACTT Films Ltd budget sheets, which reflected minimum wage agreements (BFI collection). They also draw on the 60 interviews analysed and on the 1931 and 1951 censuses of occupational classifications.

below-the-line positions were the domain of male workers with shared craft identities (Christopherson & Storper, 1989), ignoring the variety of trades in film production. In the UK context, making distinctions between the five grades, the four occupational categories and the important role HODs played in the employment relationship provides a richer picture of BTL employment. This employment incorporated a number of female-dominated occupations and departments, such as continuity, wardrobe and hair and make-up.

Table 2: Emerging 'professions' in film production, 1931-1951

1931 Census: 'Film Producers, Film Studio Managers'	1951 Census: 'Producers and Stage managers in Film studios'
	Art Advisor (Film Production)
Cinema Art Expert	Art Director (Films)
	Casting Director (Films)
	Chief cameraman (Films)
	Constructional Manager (Film sets)
Director of Production	Director of Production
	Director of Sound Recording
	Dubbing Editor
	Film Director
Film Editor	Editor
	Studio Manager
	First assistant Director
	Production Manager

Source: Census (1931 and 1951): ORDER XXI – PERSONS PROFESSIONALLY ENGAGED IN ENTERTAINMENTS AND SPORT, Classifications of Occupations (England and Wales) HMSO.

Employment flexibility in a two-tier studio system

While labour market dualism partly explains the different types of employment and lengths of job tenure in the two-tier studio system, with 'core' workers seemingly protected by permanent contracts in the larger studios and 'peripheral' workers on temporary contracts in the smaller studios, the data here suggest a more complex picture. Large studios awarded both permanent and temporary contracts and the volatile nature of the market meant that even workers on permanent contracts were susceptible to unemployment during sector-wide downturns in production. The degree of employment casualisation also varied by occupation. Nevertheless, on the whole, employment over the period appears to have been more secure than today, despite the two-tier studio system.

The number of permanent staff in a studio was dependent on the size of the in-house production company that ran it. A large studio would hire several film units across departments. Each unit consisted of a crew made up of sound, camera and production lighting technicians. In general, the 25 studios in London and the South East kept a small number of permanent technicians and production office workers in these units, and hired additional temporary workers when required. Craft and design workers were not employed in units, but were hired as required on temporary contracts during busy production periods. A production manager at Elstree explains:

> ...it was quite extraordinary the way that departments were run with the absolute minimum personnel [...] with so much going on, so few people were really at the top....you realise that the actual heads of departments and key personnel at Elstree, where five pictures might be on the go, was probably about twelve people, you know.[13]

Most of the studios operating in this period had a very small permanent staff, keeping a second group in the art department, production lighting, sound, camera and production office, on week-long rolling contracts. These could continue for several years but were sometimes terminated during downturns in production with staff being rehired later. Eddie Dryhurst worked as a script editor at Wembley, a medium sized studio owned by the US 'major', Fox in the 1930s:

> I worked on a weekly basis, I was paid a weekly salary and a week's notice on either side sort of thing. And we used to go on month after month, year after year, but we were not under contract.[14]

Sometimes staff on permanent contracts were 'hired out' or 'loaned' to other studios when there was a downturn in production at their studio, allowing employers to retain their skills. Some workers had jobs outside film, while others had two jobs in the industry. An ACT report in 1935 confirmed that many members were unable to maintain employment throughout the year (Reid, 2008). When production declined or in-house studios closed, 'core' workers on temporary contracts were released either to search for casual employment with independent production companies, making 'quota quickies', or to work in other industries, thus joining the peripheral sections of the film labour market.

Traditional craft workers were on particularly insecure contracts, some with just two hours notice, and often had to wait outside studio gates to get daily work. This improved slightly during the 1930s with NATKE and the ETU signing a series of individual studio agreements over contracts, but until the national agreements in 1947 these remained insecure. Gus Walker started as a carpenter at Denham when it was being built in 1935 and rose up the hierarchy there, then moved to Pinewood to work for the Rank Organisation, becoming a studio construction manager by the 1950s:

> In the early days [...] people worked on Elstree and different places on daily rate, you could be called for a day. They used to wait outside the gate. That didn't happen at Denham; you were hired by the week, but the thing is you could get two hours notice. This operated until the big agreement was made, but prior to that you were on two hours notice.[15]

Walker's career was more stable than most craft workers and he was able to establish himself as a permanent worker after World War Two. By the 1950s he was confident

---

13   EM Smedley-Aston (b1912-2006) BHP Interview 407 (Transcription): conducted by Roy Fowler and Mary Harvey (1997).
14   Eddie Dryhurst (b1908-1989) BHP Interview 36 (transcription): Conducted by Roy Fowler (1988)
15   Gus Walker (b1913) BHP Interview 278 (Audio Recording): Conducted by Joyce Robinson (2000)

enough of obtaining work to become a freelancer and in the 1970s started his own rigging company. But for many other craft workers careers were more precarious. Les Hillings, a stagehand who started at GBPC Shepherds Bush in 1932, was laid off in the mid-1930s and, unable to find enough film work to support his family, became a bus driver in 1937. After the war, he returned to production until 1952, when he found secure full-time employment as a laboratory technician in post-production. He explains the nature of employment in the 1930s:

> Well it's not freelance in the true sense of the word, its no – freelance, it sounds nice – [...] it invariably went, if the picture was finished you were finished as well, just went without saying you know. [Someone] come round on a Friday afternoon and they'd say 'sorry mate, you're finishing tonight'. One accepted that. It was just a run of the mill thing. This is what happened. [If...] a picture was about to start at Elstree or Ealing or Twickenham. [We would...] get there early in the morning, stand outside hoping somebody would come out and say: 'any props, any stage hands, any chippies[16].[17]

Tilly Day was on freelance contracts throughout her career from 1917 to 1975. She had been working occasionally in the industry as a secretary and a film extra, moving back to secretarial roles in other industries when there was no work in film until she secured more regular work on low budget 'quota quickies' in the 1930s. This allowed Day to move into continuity and establish her career. When work was available in studios she would take it, sometimes working all night and through the next day and also facing periods without work. Many women were obliged to build their careers against this uncertainty in the 1930s. It is important however to see film production work in relation to the lack of wider opportunities for women in this period. Day comments:

> Well, in my lifetime if you were a girl – nobody ever said to you, 'What are you going to do when you grow up?' Because there wasn't anything that you could do, barring get married.[18]

Employment contracts were thus largely casual and short-term, although some workers had long job tenure in the same department. These departments developed formal bureaucracies, in contrast with the contemporary industry structure (Eikhof & Warhurst, 2013). Contrary to general accounts of insecure employment in the industries, these formal bureaucracies did in fact create some 'traditional careers' (Jones 1997). Some of the workers with secure employment were employed by the Rank Organisation or Ealing Studios under the charge of Michael Balcon between1938 and 1959, but the majority of workers in the archive who had long-term employment in the same studio were those who moved into TV production in the post-war period.

Entry routes and network intelligence

Analysis demonstrates varied entry routes during this period, with different patterns emerging in each of the four occupational categories. Of the 31 production office

---

16   'Chippy' is a slang term for a carpenter.
17   Les Hilling (b1914) BHP interview 274 (audio recording): Conducted by Alan Lawson and Syd Wilson (1993).
18   Tilly Day. Extra, secretary and 'Continuity Girl' (b1903-1994) BHP Interview 30 (transcribed): Conducted by Sid Cole and Alan Lawson (1988).

workers and technicians in the sound and camera departments, 22 were male, a small number of whom were electrical engineering workers who moved from maintenance and lighting into sound and camera departments. Some entered through the Regents Park Technical College, which offered vocational film courses in the 1930s. The rest started as paid interns, getting in through an introduction to the studio, either from a family contact or an 'old boy' contact from private school who knew someone in a senior position in the organisation (a studio manager or a highly regarded HOD on a permanent contract). These entrants became trainees in an 'informal apprenticeship' system (Reid, 2008) which continued after 1947. Sound, camera and production office training, with low pay and no guarantee of future employment or even vocational certification, formed a barrier for many more economically-marginal aspirants. These departments had a large proportion of middle-class entrants, educated in private schools, a majority of whom were male, a proportion which increased further up the production hierarchy.

Of the eleven male workers in the craft trades (in studio construction and lighting departments) one came via the theatre, while the remaining ten entered as the new studios were built and others converted to sound stages. They gained their skills through vocational courses and work in industries such as construction, shipbuilding and electrical engineering, developing a high level of skill before they entered the film industry. They had a film industry contact further down the employment hierarchy, often gaining employment after hearing about temporary employment from a studio craft worker or lighting electrician (in Grade 4) with whom they had worked in another industry. Without a contact in a high grade in the industry to act as a mentor, they were dependent on more senior members in their department to recommend them for promotion or further employment, often based on their technical proficiency and speed of performance. By the mid-1930s, agreements between employers and the ETU and NAT(K)E meant that union membership was essential for entry. However entry was not enough in itself: sustaining employment in the industry was still dependent on informal relationships with senior core workers and HODs.

Of the sample, 15 were women, of whom six were designers in art departments (hair, wardrobe and production design) who entered through formal training via the theatre, the fashion industry or the Architectural Association. This provided them with status before they entered the film industry and enabled them to progress in those departments where relatively well-paid careers for women were possible, though the number of jobs available was still small.

The remaining nine female interviewees began their careers as production secretaries. All had received training in shorthand and typing at schools such as the Pitman College and accessed employment through a variety of routes. They would assist male producers with shooting scripts, getting an insight into the film-making process from its conception. Some moved on into other areas of production such as continuity, seen from the 1930s to the 1960s as 'women's work'. Four of the nine production secretaries (Grade 4) progressed to Grades 1 and 2 in production. As they explain in their interviews, they were a minority in these high grades. The production secretaries would also keep each other informed of any jobs in continuity or on the production floor when new film projects were in early stages of development. This follows a similar pattern to the early networks in the studios at this time, where workers in the more precarious trades developed contacts and shared labour market intelligence.

Between 1927 and 1947 the network of family dynasties that emerged in later decades had not yet been established, so the nepotism that is often attributed to the industry was not a central factor in determining entry. However many workers spoke of 'getting an introduction' into the industry through informal family contacts, private school contacts, (via relatives who were employers in the studios) or from work colleagues in prior employment (who knew a HOD or a 'core' worker in a studio). Interviewees mention getting their children and other relatives into the film industry in the post-war period. This is significant because union membership was the only way to gain access and could only be obtained after two recommendations from existing members. However, despite the fact that entry routes before the post-war closed shop era were more varied, favoured entry through informal networks was still prominent, especially for those who went on to reach the top two grades in the industry. Informal contacts were therefore an important entry route for workers in this period and remain so today.

Training

Craft workers and designers in the 'traditional' trades (the art departments, studio construction and production lighting) received their training in other industries, and had to adapt to the particular requirements in the film industry on the job. In the specialised film trades, the production office, camera and sound departments, it was accepted that some form of training was necessary. In the late 1920s and 1930s the HODs in many of the highest pay grades were often technicians from Germany, Italy, Hungary and, more often, the USA. As these studio departments were emerging, the early HODs trained many of the first generation of UK technicians using an on-the-job approach, where many were expected to 'sink or swim' and there was little room for structured programmes – a system of training which continues today in semi-permanent work groups (Reid, 2008).

In the 1930s, the ACT attempted to get employers' federations to agree to formal apprenticeships for technicians in sound and camera; however the uncertainty of the industry formed an obstacle and training remained informal. The studios employed a number of interns known as 'number boys', 'clapper boys' or 'office boys' on wages that were below the national average. These interns would be engaged in some technical work and general studio duties. Of the 12 interviewees who began as low-paid trainees eleven had been to private schools and only one, the cinematographer Jack Cardiff, went to an elementary school. During their internships they would work anything from 60 to 100 hours a week, often late into the night. The majority got in through a family contact, who would often act as a protective mentor in their early careers. Significantly, they all eventually moved into Grade 1 and 2 positions and eight moved into above-the-line creative 'talent' positions. Trainees were generally used as cheap labour rather than being part of a structured training scheme. Hugh Stewart started as a trainee at GBPC Shepherds Bush in 1932, through his mother's contact with Ian Dalrymple, an editor who went on to run Warwick Films (one of Rank's 'Independents') in the 1940s. Stewart underwent one of the few official training programmes as the studio departments were emerging, but was not impressed:

> ...we were just pushed into the place and made assistants and sidekicks and that kind of thing [...] we were given a princely salary of five bob[19] a week. And then after three months we got ten bob a week and then for the last six months we were told we would get ... for those who were still existing, and by this time there were about ten of us... we got a pound a week.[20]

Dalrymple played the role of mentor in Stewart's early career and acted as a powerful protector, ensuring that he was given an early pay increase and recommending that he should be given an editing credit on the Hitchcock film *The Man Who Knew Too Much* (1933). This distinguished credit and the recommendation from Dalrymple were the springboard for Stewart's future freelance career as an editor and producer.

Despite their initially low wages, long hours, poor working conditions and poor training programmes, those that remained and showed aptitude could often expect a secure future. As one trainee and future film producer put it, 'We knew we were being exploited but we figured that in the long run it was probably all right'.[21]

This informal but extensive training provided an income and an opportunity to gain skills and experience that were of benefit to future careers which is rare today.

Working hours and the growth of labour organisation

The working week was generally long, ranging from 60 to 100 hours. In sound and camera departments the average working day was 12-15 hours and, exceptionally, the working week was seven days, with overtime pay rare. Tubby Englander started as a clapper boy at the small Cricklewood studios in 1930 and was a camera assistant at the larger GBPC Shepherds Bush by the mid-1930s:

> Finishing times were purely arbitrary. You could go on until 10 o'clock at night. You could finish at 7 o'clock at night, and sometimes you could work all night and half the next day. And of course the same goes for weekends; you could work seven days a week if necessary. More often than not you never worked five, you always worked six. Saturday was part and parcel of the week.[22]

Self-employed workers like Englander were not paid overtime and were often obliged to work long hours. Craft workers were on a flat 48-52 hour working week, and then paid overtime as NATKE and the ETU made studio agreements throughout the 1930s. A sound technician at the small Nettlefolds studios in the early 1930s explains:

> What they did do of course, they worked the studio staff [...] So the overtime was used a hell of a lot, but the technicians, we got no overtime. The 'sparks'[23] did, the

---

19   'Five bob' is a slang term for five shillings – the equivalent of 25 pence (or 25% of a pound) in decimal currency. 'Ten bob' was ten shillings, or 50 pence. In present-day equivalents, 5 'bob' (shillings) = £68 and one pound (£1) = £272, using the 'income status' measurement on the Measuring Worth website: see bibliography.

20   Hugh Stewart: assistant editor, editor, producer (b1910) BHP Interview 108 (transcribed): Conducted by John Legard and Alan Lawson (1988).

21   EM Smedley Aston Ibid.

22   Tubby Englander (b1916-2004) BHP Interview 22 (transcribed): Conducted by Arthur Graham and Dave Robson (1987)

23   'Spark' is a slang term for an electrician

> workmen, but the technicians got nothing. We could work every night until one o'clock in the morning. If you were lucky you got a bottle of ginger beer and a sandwich.[24]

The working week was therefore longer than the national average, with unsociable hours expected, bearing comparison with film production today. In the 1930s, workers in film units were often paid a weekly salary and no overtime. This type of unpaid labour was one of the main grievances among non-unionised workers and is a reason they organised, as an art director and early ACT member, who joined in 1933 explains:

Rodney Giesler: *Can you describe the sort of things that prompted the formation of the union? I mean, why were you involved in the formation of it?*

L.P Williams (Art Director): *...well of course one was young and enthusiastic, and that sort of thing, so one didn't mind much. But one did get rather fed up with the hours that were worked. And I think that's what we thought needed putting right. [...] especially when work, as usual in the British film industry, wasn't all that plentiful, and so if you got a job, you weren't likely to kick up a row about it [...] Me and Freddie Young [DOP] used to go up to London for [union] meetings in the evening.* [25]

Because the ACT was not recognised by employers in the early 1930s, members would have secret committee meetings in cafes and pubs[26] and recruit colleagues while working alongside them. Tilly Day was recruited to the ACT by the head of her film unit at Stoll Studios, Cricklewood:

> Desmond Dickinson was number four, his [union] card was number four and he said, 'You must join this, Tilly, because it's gonna be a great thing, and you'll need it' [...], he persuaded me and I joined[27]

Between 1934 and 1936, ACT membership grew from eight to 1,212 (Jones, 1987).

Conclusion

Recognition of the continuities as well as the discontinuities in their historical development is missing from current appreciations of work in the creative industries. Our understanding of the employment relationship, in particular, has suffered from a tendency to pose the past only in contrast to the present, while it also bears comparison with it.

The film industry was already a global industry, dominated by US companies, by the 1920s. Attempts by the UK government to protect its national industry resulted in growth in both employment and trade union power which provided a protective shield over workers in what was, as it still is, a highly competitive labour market.

The UK film production sector did not see a dramatic shift from Fordist to post-Fordist employment practices. The decline of UK studio production was a gradual and uneven process and changes to the employment relationship are better understood

---

24 Vernon Sewell: Assistant sound technician, writer and director (b1903-2001). BHP Interview 329 (transcript) conducted by Roy Fowler (1994)

25 L.P Williams, Art Director from 1928-1960s, and early ACT activist, BHP Interview 295 (transcribed). Conducted by Rodney Giesler (1993)

26 George Elvin, General Secretary of ACT(T) 1934 to 1969, BHP transcribed recording 115 (circa 1960s)

27 Tilly Day

as a result of the weakening of labour organisation rather than simply as changes in industrial structure. The labour/capital pact lasting from 1947 to1990, which immediately followed the period described in this article, improved employment conditions and increased union control over the supply of labour, which, apart from a short period during World War Two, has always outstripped demand. Les Hillings, who commented 'it's not freelance... freelance sounds nice', makes a pertinent point: that the term 'freelance' can be a euphemism, a way of dignifying what would otherwise be recognised simply as casual or precarious labour.

Political economy provides a lens through which to view the way domestic state intervention and global capitalism can impact on workers. Combining this with archived interviews, provides a more holistic approach to understanding how this 'bigger picture' (Mosco, 2009) was experienced by workers in the lower echelons of film production, both in terms of employment conditions and in the way they responded to them. The oral histories in the BHP archive reveal that issues relating to unpaid labour, uncertain employment and long working days were common features of the experience of work in film production. In the 1930s, labour organisation was growing, with previously unorganised occupations following the path of craft workers and forming the trade union, ACT, which led to changes in the employment relationship benefiting labour. In an industry where 'structured uncertainty' (Randle & Culkin, 2009) remains a constant theme of the employment relationship, labour organisation allowed workers to gain more certainty in the post-war era. In describing employment relations in UK film in both the 1930s and the present, the term 'casualised' may be more appropriate than 'flexible'. In this sense the assertion that the advances made by labour in the post-war era were a 'great exception to a general rule' (Huws, 2011:2) appears to be confirmed by the film industry.

© Will Atkinson and Keith Randle, 2014

REFERENCES

Aksoy, A., & K. Robins (1992) 'Hollywood for the 21st century: global competition for critical mass in image markets', *Cambridge Journal of Economics,* 16(1):1-22.

Banks, M. (2010) 'Craft labour and creative industries', *International Journal of Cultural Policy,* 16(3):305–321

BECTU History Project [online]. Available from: www.bectu.org.uk/advice-resources/history-project (last accessed April, 2014)

Blair, H., N. Culkin & K. Randle (2003) 'From London to Los Angeles: a comparison of local labour market processes in the US and UK film industries', *International Journal of Human Resource Management,* 14(4):619-633

Blair, H., S. Grey& K. Randle (2001) 'Working in Film: Employment in a project based industry', *Personnel Review,* 30(2):170-185

Blair, H. (2001) 'You're Only as Good as your last Job', *Work, Employment and Society,* 15 (1):149-169

Blair, H. & A. Rainnie (2000), 'Flexible films?', *Media, Culture and Society,* 22(2):187-204

Chanan, M. (1976) *Labour Power in the British Film Industry,* London: BFI Publishing.

Christopherson, S. & M. Storper (1986) 'Flexible Specialization and Regional Industrial Agglomerations: The case of the U.S. Motion Picture Industry', *Annals of the Association of American Geographers* 77(1):104-117

Christopherson, S. & M. Storper, M. (1989) 'The Effects of Flexible Specialization on Industrial Politics and the Labor Market: The Motion Picture Industry', *Industrial and Labor Relations Review,* 42(3): 331-47.

CreativeSkillset, Job Roles [online]. Available from: http://creativeskillset.org/creative_industries/film/job_roles (last accessed, April, 2014)

Dawson, A. & S. Holmes (2012) *Working in the Global Film and Television Industries,* London: Bloomsbury.

Dawson, A. (2012) 'Labouring in Hollywood's motion picture industry and the legacy of flexible specialization' in A. Dawson & S. Holmes (eds) *Working in the Global Film and Television Industries,* London: Bloomsbury.

Doeringer, P. & M. Piore (1971) *Internal labor markets and manpower analysis,* Lexington, Massachusetts: DC Heath.

Doogan, K. (2009) *New Capitalism? The transformation of work,* Cambridge: Polity Press.

Ellis, J. (1982) *Visible Fictions,* London: Routledge.

Eikhof, D. R., & C. Warhurst (2013) 'The promised land? Why social inequalities are systemic in the creative industries', *Employee Relations,* 35(5):495-508.

Florida, R. (2002) *The Rise of the Creative Class,* New York: Basic Books.

Grugulis, I. & S. Stoyanou (2009) 'I don't know where you learn from: Skills in Film and TV', A. Mckinley & C. Smith (eds) *Creative Labour,* London: Palgrave McMillan.

Grugrulis, I. & D. Stoyanova (2012) 'Social Capital and Networks in Film and TV: Jobs for the Boys?' *Organization Studies,* 33(10): 1311-1331

Guback, T. H. (1969) *The international film industry: Western Europe and America since 1945,* USA: Indiana University Press.

Hauptmeier, M. & M. Vidal (2014), *Comparative Political Economy of Work,* London: Palgrave McMillan.

Heaton, J. (2004) *Reworking Qualitative Data,* London: Sage Publications.

Huws, U. (2011) 'Passing the buck: corporate restructing and the casualisation of employment', *Work Organisation, Labour and Globalisation,* 5(1):1-9.

Jones, C. (1996) 'Careers in Project Networks: The Case of the Film Industry', M.B Arthur & D.M. Rousseau (eds) *The Boundaryless Career: A New Employment Principle for a New Organizational Era,* New York & Oxford: Oxford University Press.

Jones, S. (1987) *The British Labour Movement and Film, 1918-1939,* London: Routledge.

Kelly, T. (1966) *A Competitive Cinema,* London: The Institute of Economic Affairs.

Officer, L.H & S. Williamson (2014) 'Six Ways to Compute the Relative Value of a UK pound amount, 1270 to present. *Measuring Worth,* 2014 [online] http://www.measuringworth.com/ukcompare/ (last accessed April 2014)

Lee, D. (2011) 'Networks, cultural capital and creative labour in the British independent television sector', *Media, Culture and Society,* 33 (4): 549-565

Low, R. (1985) *The History of the British Film 1929-1939: Film Making in 1930s Britain,* London: George Allen and Unwin.

McKinlay, A. & C. Smith (2009) *Creative Labour: Working in the Creative Industries,* London: Palgrave MacMillan.

Mayer, V. (2011) *Below The Line: Producers and Production Studies in the New Television Economy,* Durham, North Carolina: Duke University Press.

Mosco, V. (2009) *The Political Economy of Communication,* (2nd edition) London: Sage Publications.

Nielson, M. (1983) 'Towards a workers' history of the U.S. Film industry', V. Mosco & J. Wasko (eds) *Labor, the working class, and the media* (Vol. 1), Norwood, NJ: Ablex Publishing.

Percival, N., & D. Hesmondhalgh (2014) 'Unpaid work in the UK television and film industries: Resistance and changing attitudes', *European Journal of Communication,* 29(2): 1-16

Piore, J. & F.C. Sabel (1984) *The Second Industrial Divide,* New York: Basic Books.

Porter, V. (1983) 'The Context of Creativity: Ealing Studios and Hammer Films', J.Curran & V. & Porter (eds) *British Cinema History,* Paramus, NJ: Barnes and Noble.

Powdermaker, H. (1950), *Hollywood: The Dream Factory (An Anthropologist looks at the Movie-Makers)* New York: Little, Brown and Company.

Randle, K, W.F. Leung & J. Kurian (2008) *Creating Difference: Overcoming Barriers to Diversity in UK Film and Television Employment,* Research Report for the European Social Fund.

Reid, I. (2008) *The persistence of the internal labour market in changing circumstances: the British film production industry during and after the closed shop*. PhD Thesis, London School of Economics.

Ryan, B. (1991) 'Making Capital from Culture', *de Gruyter studies in Organisation*, 35.

Sargent-Disc (2011) *Age and Gender in UK film industry* [online] Available from: www.sargent-disc.com/sargent-disc-uk/news-insights/insights/uk-film-industry-age-and-gender.aspx (last accessed April 2014)

Scott, A. (2002) 'A new map of Hollywood: the production and distribution of American motion pictures', *Regional Studies*, 36(9):957-975

Sparks, C. (1994) 'Independent Production: Unions and Casualization' , Hood, S. (ed) *Behind The Screens*, London: Lawrence and Wishart.

Stall, M. (2009) 'Privilege and Distinction in Production Worlds', M.J. Banks, J.T. Caldwell & V. Mayer (ed) *Production Studies: Cultural Studies of Media Industries*, New York: Routledge.

Standing, G. (2011), *The Precariat: the new dangerous class*, London: Bloomsbury Publishing.

Staiger, J. (1985) 'The Hollywood Mode of Production to 1930', D. Bordwell, J, Staiger & K. Thompson (eds) *The Classical Mode of Production*, London: Routledge.

Street, S. (1997) *British National Cinema*, London: Routledge.

Threadgall, D. (1994) *Shepperton Studios: an independent view*, London: BFI Publishing.

Wakso, J. (2003) *How Hollywood Works*, London: Sage.

Wayne, M. (2003) *Marxism and Media Studies: Key Concepts and Trends*, London: Pluto Press.

Wood, L. (1997) 'Low-budget Films in the 1930s', R. Murphy (ed), *The British Cinema Book*. London: BFI Publishing.

Wood, L. (1986) *British Films 1927-1939*, London: BFI Publishing.

Old wine, new bottles and the Internet

Guglielmo Carchedi

Guglielmo Carchedi is Professor Emeritus at the University of Amsterdam, Netherlands, and Adjunct Professor at York University, Toronto, Canada.

ABSTRACT

The Internet has given a new shape to modern capitalism. These new features have drawn the attention of numerous scholars and have become the focus of highly topical and controversial questions. However, as a rule, the literature has not taken as its starting point the development of a Marxist epistemology. The reason for this is the failure to derive a Marxist theory of knowledge from Marx's value theory. This is the task this article sets itself. The first section conceptualises mental versus objective labour processes and rejects the notion of the non-materiality of knowledge. The second section builds on this conceptualisation and deals with three interrelated questions, namely whether mental labour can produce value and surplus value and whether the distinctions on the one hand between productive and unproductive labour and on the other between production and consumption retain their validity in mental production. The third section explores the class nature of knowledge with particular reference to the Internet. Some final considerations follow in the last section.

Some elements of a Marxist epistemology[1]

Consider labour. It is a transformative process, that is, a sequence of transformations. These can be of two types: objective transformations and mental transformations.

Objective transformations transform objective reality, reality that exists outside of our perception, even if we need to perceive it in order to transform it. More precisely:

(1) $OT = L \rightarrow (MO, OO) = ON$

where OT is objective transformations whose outcome is ON, the new objective use values, or output; L is labour power; MO are the objective means of objective transformations (e.g. a hammer); and OO is the objective objects of objective transformations (e.g. marble). The symbol -> indicates transformations. L transforms the terms within parentheses. The outcome is ON.

In mental transformations, labour power transforms its own knowledge and therefore

---

1   For a more complete analysis see Carchedi, 2012, chapters 1 and 4. See also Carchedi, 2005.

itself. This is why KL appears in both parentheses, both the transforming and the transformed elements. Labour power also transforms the knowledge contained in objective reality (e.g. books or computers) into new knowledge:

(2) MT = (L, KL)-> (KL, KO) = KN

where MT is mental transformations whose outcome is new knowledge, KN. KL is the knowledge existing in labour power and KO is the knowledge contained in objective sources of knowledge (books, computers) outside KL. KL is both the mental means of mental transformations and one of the two mental objects of mental transformation (it transforms itself), the other one being KO. KL as one of the inputs of a mental transformation is not the same as its output, KN, because KN is the outcome of the combination of L, KL, and KO (the inputs). Since KN is immediately incorporated into KL, KN as the output of one MT becomes immediately the KL of the next mental transformation.[2]

It would be mistaken to consider mental transformations as 'immaterial'. Both objective and mental transformations are material. In fact, both require the expenditure of human energy, which is material, as shown by human metabolism. More specifically, the expenditure of human energy that constitutes the cognitive process, thinking, causes a change in the nervous system, in the interconnections between the neurons of the brain. This is called synapsis. It is these changes that make possible a different perception of the world. Knowledge, even if intangible, is thus material. To deny this means to ignore the results of neuroscience. After all, if electricity and its effects are material, why should the electrical activity of the brain and its effects (knowledge) not also be material? There is no 'immaterial' labour, *pace* the workerist authors.[3] But of course, while synapses make possible (changed) perceptions of the world, what is perceived is eminently social; it is the myriad social relations and processes in all their infinite manifestations constituting a society. *Knowledge is always both material and social.*

The question of the (im)materiality of knowledge is of the utmost importance for value theory.[4] If knowledge were immaterial, its production could not produce something material, value. Since it is material, it can produce value and surplus value. But under what conditions?

Transformations are transformations of use values. In (1) the use values that are transformed are *objective use values*, M^O and O^O. In (2) the use values that are transformed are *mental use values*: the use value of specific forms of knowledge; the use to which a form of knowledge lends itself. The mental use values transformed by labour power are K^L and K^O.

The distinction between the two types of transformations is only analytical because in reality objective transformations require mental transformations and vice versa. However, this distinction is necessary to conceptualise the labour process and thus labour. A labour process is always the transformation of use values, both objective and mental. But it is

---

[2] This is the temporalist approach whose application solves the so-called transformation problem. See Carchedi, 1984, 2001 and 2012.
[3] A complete critique of workerism is beyond the scope of this work. See Carchedi, 2012; Henninger, 2007, Starosta, 2012. For some authors, especially of a workerist persuasion, the notion of 'immaterial' seems to resemble that of 'mental' in this work. Even so, the gulf is unbridgeable because workerism rejects Marx's labour theory of value while the present work retains it and builds a Marxist epistemology upon it.
[4] And, as we shall see, class determined.

either objective or mental according to which type of transformation is determinant. The relation of determination would require a detailed analysis.[5] Here suffice it to mention that to be determinant means to be the condition of existence of the determined instance and to be determined means to be the condition of reproduction or supersession of the determinant instance. Then, the objective labour process is:

(3) OLP = (OT => MT) = ON
where ON, the objective product, is the result of the objective labour process (OLP), the interaction of objective and mental transformations in which the former determine the latter. It is thus mistaken to think that objective labour, sometimes called physical or manual or material labour, is separated from mental activity.[6]

In the mental labour process (MLP), the mental transformations are determinant:

(4) MLP = (MT => OT) = KN
where KN is new knowledge. KN has been considered to be the outcome only of mental transformations, as in (2) above, only as a first approximation. In reality, KN is the outcome of a mental labour process that requires both mental and objective transformations. For example, the production of a video game (MLP) requires an objective transformation, say the transformation of white paper into printed paper through a printer. The printer is an objective means of objective transformations. But within the context of an MLP, it is also an objective means of a mental labour process, a condition for the (re)production of that form of knowledge, the video game.

Three points follow from this. First, knowledge as an input of the MLP is not the output of that process.[7] Second, new knowledge is not necessarily different knowledge. It is knowledge produced anew, even if it is a replica of an old one. Third, the key to distinguish an objective from a mental labour process is whether in general it is used for its objective content (e.g. a shoe) or its mental content (e.g. a book).

Value and the Internet

The social determination of the Internet as a web of computers and as a technique of treating information is well known: it originated in the Cold War.[8] Generally speaking, this is not the focus of dispute. Rather, the controversy hinges upon whether Marx's value theory is still valid under modern conditions. Two preliminary points should be made.

First, within capitalism, the labour process (either mental or objective) is one of two aspects of the *production process*, the other one being the *surplus value producing process*, or exploitation. This latter means that labourers must transform objective or mental use values for a time longer than that necessary for the production of their socially determined means of objective or mental consumption. Thus, a part of the

---

5   See Carchedi, 2012, especially chapter 1.
6   Rey (2012:406) is one of many holding this view.
7   There is no circularity but a succession of MLPs. This is different from the view that 'Information is circular, in the sense that it is both input and output . . . therefore it becomes very difficult to distinguish production, distribution and consumption of information.' (Kostakis, 2012: 2). This comes very close to arguing that information is both the input and the output of the same MLP, a mistake made by a great number of authors, Marxist and non-Marxist alike, especially when dealing with the transformation of values into prices.
8   See e.g. Denton, P.H. & S. Restivo (2008:160-171).

working day must be used to produce objective or mental use values for the capitalists. To this end, labourers must be forced to deliver surplus labour by those agents who, as Marx says in vol. III of *Capital*, perform the *function of capital* (or work of control and surveillance) without being capitalists, without being the owners of the means of objective or mental production.⁹ If labourers internalise the desirability of providing surplus labour, they internalise the function of capital. As we shall see, nowadays this latter option is more easily applicable to certain types of mental labourers, also on the Internet.

Second, in dealing with the Internet, we should distinguish between three categories of *mental producers,* those who I have referred to above, as a first approximation, mental labourers.

The first of these categories consists of those mental producers who use the Internet to work for capital. They are the *mental labourers* proper.

The second consists of those mental producers who use the Internet for profit without being capitalists. They are the *mental self-employed*. They will not be dealt with here both for reasons of space and because they are the debris originating from the collision between the two basic classes.

The third category consists of those mental producers who use the Internet for other purposes (for recreation, education, research, etc.) while not working for capital, but in their own free time. I refer to this group as *mental agents*, the producers of knowledge free from the rule of capital.¹⁰ It is important to keep in mind the distinction between mental labourers and mental agents, since this distinction is essential to review the three questions debated in the literature.

Do mental labourers on the Internet produce surplus value?
The first question is *whether mental labourers on the Internet produce value*. Since value is labour expended under the capitalist production relation (by labour for capital), the production of knowledge (mental labour) can be productive of value and surplus value because it is mental labour performed for capital. In this case, the quantity of new value generated during the mental labour process is given by the length and intensity of the abstract mental labour performed, given the value of the labour power of the mental labourers. Exploitation, then, is the difference between the value of the mental labourers' labour power and the value they generate. This value might be incorporated in an objective shell or not. In both cases it is an intangible but material commodity whose value is determined by the quantity of mental labour needed to produce it.¹¹

Besides these general features, mental production on the Internet has its own specificities, namely new labour processes, new positions, and new forms of exploitation. But these specificities do not cancel their capitalist nature. Let us take the example of a new labour process studied by Legault (Legault, 2013:84): the production

---

9   The notion of ownership of the means of mental production will be dealt with further down.
10 In the literature they are referred to as users. But they are not simply users. They are producers of knowledge. They use, consume, pre-existing knowledge as an input of the process of mental production.
11 As Pfeiffer correctly remarks, 'in the present state of research, no clear and conclusive statement can be made that the source of value creation has actually changed.' (2013: 19).

of video games.¹² Since each video game is a unique piece and the technologies change rapidly, some of the personnel are highly skilled; but not all of them. Capital stamps the structure of the labour process by creating a bureaucratic hierarchy that includes more as well as less qualified tasks. The function of capital as brute external coercion, as in the Tayloristic assembly line, is ill suited for the control of the personnel whose labour relies on their relatively spontaneous creativity. In this case, new ways to control labour are necessary. The capitalists, through the supervisors (project managers), see to it that their labourers complete their tasks within the time allocated to them. Project managers monitor the developers' progress and pay them when the project has reached some important points (milestones). The labourers are controlled by project managers who have internalised the aims and rationality of capital. But within these limits, labourers are free to take their own decisions and set their pace of work. Control has changed semblance. But this neither cancels exploitation nor frees labour from capital's rule.

Thus, the greater autonomy of these highly qualified mental labourers is far from being absolute. Flexible and intellectually and emotionally rewarding labour hides long working hours, long and frequent hours of unpaid overtime (Legault, 2013:79) and the maximisation of labour intensity (Pitts, 2013:102). Terranovea (2000) refers to America Online (AOL) as an 'electronic sweatshop.' Moreover, these positions are subjected to tendential dequalification.¹³ It is not only, as Pitts aptly puts it, 'disciplined autonomy' (Pitts, 2013:101). It is also creativity moulded by capital. Capital pays labourers to be creative, but this creativity must be consonant with capital's aims and not with the labourers' full and all-round development.

New divisions of tasks emerge. For example, some of the labourers working for search engines analyse blogs, both quantitatively in terms of the number of visitors, and qualitatively in terms of the comments left by the visitors and thus in terms of their ideas, preferences, etc. Other labourers navigate the web looking for ideas helpful for advertising campaigns, for example by analysing chat lines. Still others transform this material into a commodity to be sold to advertising agencies.

Some commentators have emphasised another aspect: the blurring of the frontier between working time and private life. For example, labourers solve 'creative problems' regarding their jobs in their free time (Pitts, 2013:95). Or, labourers can answer emails or keep up their correspondence with bloggers from home, also in their free time. The question is whether this labour is productive of value. If capital is a relation of production, this relation is *suspended* in the labourer's free time and *resumed* when the labourers return to their work. In the time they work at home they do not produce *value* because during this time they are not paid by capital. Rather, they produce *use values*. When they return to their work, it is as if they answered those emails in the

---

12   For a thorough analysis of the production of video games see Dyer-Witheford & de Peute, 2009. This is a valuable work, in spite of its reliance on the workerist perspective, in that it highlights the interaction of virtual games and the social context within which they are developed.

13   As an anonymous referee has remarked, 'Initially ... software developers could partly pursue non-economic goals such as actually writing the best software for a certain problem (focus on use values). With growing competition this is no longer the case: now they have to find a solution that ... creates the lowest costs (focus on exchange values).'

first instant of their work. It is as if they worked more intensely. The capitalists increase their profits because of that increased intensity. It follows that the extra surplus value must be appropriated from the competitors through the price mechanism.

Critics hold that the productivity of mental production cannot be measured. But consider first objective production. Productivity is measured as units of output per unit of capital invested. This holds also for mental production, say, a video game. Consider first the numerator. The mental product can be contained in a physical shell (a DVD). The DVDs produced can be counted as units of output. But the videogame can also be downloaded from one computer to another. The number of downloads can also be counted. They, too, are units of output. In short, the mental output can be counted because it is material. This is the numerator.

As for the denominator, consider first the capital invested in the *prototype*. This is not only fixed constant capital (computers, premises, facilities, chips foundries, assembly plants, etc.). It is also circulating constant capital (raw materials) and variable capital (wages). Then there is the capital invested in administration, pre-sale advertising and other costs. Let us call all this capital (a).

Secondly, there is the capital invested in the production and sale of the *replicas* of the prototype. This is the capital of type (a) for the production and delivery of the replicas plus the capital of type (a) for the sale of the product (e.g. advertising) during the whole life cycle of the mental labour process. Let us call the capital needed for the production and sale of the replicas (b). The total capital invested is thus (a) plus (b). This is the denominator of productivity ratio. Productivity in mental production can be computed.

Another related misconception is that the unit value of the copies is or tends (practically) to zero. In reality, the *total* value of the replicas is given by (a) plus (b) plus (c) where (c) is the surplus value generated during the whole life cycle of the mental labour process. The *unit* value is then given by the total value divided by the number of replicas made. It is directly proportional to the total value and inversely proportional to the quantity of the replicas. Then, the capital invested in the prototype is spread over an increasing number of replicas. Let us assume for the sake of argument that it is or tends towards zero. But the capital invested in the production and sale of the replicas plus the surplus value generated increase as the output increases. The unit value does not tend towards zero, *pace* the costless reproducibility of the workerist 'cognitive commodity'.

The size of this mental output is variable. It depends on the technology used. Its limit is obsolescence, a point reached when, due to intense competition, its demand falls to the point at which it is not profitable any longer to produce it. In the sectors with intense competition, as in the video games sector, this causes a high rate of business failures. If production stops when the receipts are less than the capital invested, a loss is suffered. If production continues after that point, profits are made.

What are the alternatives submitted by the critics of the application of the labour theory of value to the production of knowledge? Let us take two examples. For Jodi Dean (2010), 'Just as industrial capitalism relied on the exploitation of labor, so does communicative capitalism rely on the exploitation of communication.' In this approach, communication is reified. The point is that communication is knowledge and knowledge is the product of mental labour. Thus the exploitation of communication is simply the exploitation of the mental labourers' (abstract) mental labour.

For Arvidsson and Colleoni (2012), Marx's value theory is not applicable to the Internet. For these authors, value is the affective attachment to a commodity, to a brand. Presumably, the greater the number of customers attached to a brand (and thus buying that product), the greater its value. This is the view of the capitalists who aim at maximising their share of the market by manipulating demand, i.e. by influencing the redistribution of value. But before it can be redistributed, value must be produced. The source of value and thus of surplus value remains unexplained. Therefore this approach is useless as an economic theory. For example, the authors fail to explain how the (dis)accumulation of affective investments can explain, say, economic crises.

The above calls for some short remarks on so-called affective labour, i.e. labour that produces or manipulates affects (wrongly referred to as 'immaterial labour'). Here I am not referring to housework, which is not performed for capital and thus must be the object of a separate analysis. Rather, I mean the kinds of labour that some Autonomist authors describe as 'affective': advertising, care work, the jobs of flight attendants, fast food workers, etc. All these categories can be easily accommodated within the law of value. Advertising is an example of unproductive mental labour. Care work is an example of objective productive labour because it preserves and reconstitutes the commodity labour power (which is material). Flight attendants are an element of transportation (which for Marx is both objective and productive of value) and thus their labour is both objective and productive. And fast food workers are also productive labourers whose objective product is sold by the capitalists to customers for profit. As for friendly sales staff, whose sales figures are better than those of their less friendly colleagues, they are more skilled (whether their friendliness is a character trait or learned) and thus more efficient. Their labour power thus has a higher value. But they are unproductive workers and thus do not produce value. Through their greater efficiency and thus their higher sales, they make it possible for the commercial capitalists to appropriate more surplus value from other capitalists.

The distinction between productive and unproductive labour

The *second question* concerns the distinction between productive and unproductive labour, which is supposedly invalid in mental production and especially on the Internet.

Let us first begin with objective labour. For Marx, labour immersed in the capitalist production relation is productive if it transforms use values into new use values. It is thus unproductive in the following four cases. First, labour employed in commerce. As Marx argues, while productive labour transforms objective use values, unproductive labour deals with them without transforming them. If one exchanges objective use values, one cannot transform them. Second, labour employed in finance and speculation. This is unproductive because it does not deal at all with objective use values. Third, there are those who perform the work of control and surveillance, the function of capital. They can be called 'non-labourers'. The fact that they are necessary for the capitalist production process does not make them productive of value. They cannot produce value because one cannot transform use values if one forces others to perform that transformation.[14] Finally, the labour that destroys objective use values cannot be productive of value because it destroys the specific form (use values) in which value is contained.

Similarly, the production of knowledge by mental labourers is productive of value because it transforms mental use values. But on the basis of the above, it is not productive of value if it theorises: (a) the exchange of objective use values; (b) financing and speculation; (c) the performance of the function of capital; and (d) the destruction of objective use values.[15] The question is not whether the generation of knowledge *tout court* is productive or not.[16] The question is when it is and when it is not. The distinction between productive and unproductive mental labourers also holds if they operate through the Internet.

Let us now look at the *mental agents*.[17] They, too, are unproductive, but for a different reason, because they are not employed by capital. Consider, for example, the 'social buttons' on Facebook. The mental agents who click on social buttons ('Like', 'Share', and so on), or who discuss a variety of issues on blogs, or who develop technological innovations through their interaction, transform mental use values. At the same time, they provide knowledge to whoever is interested in it. This knowledge is free, not because it costs nothing (think of the wear and tear on the computer, of the energy consumed, etc.) but because anybody can appropriate it free of charge. On the Internet, this is what the search engines, a specific form of capitalist mental production, do through their mental labourers.[18] They transform this knowledge into marketable knowledge, i.e. they quantify data on tastes, desires, interests, etc. Then they sell this data to other capitalists who use it to plan advertising campaigns and investments, to evaluate the credit-worthiness of clients, and so on. Those capitalists that are more skilful in appropriating the knowledge generated by the mental agents (so-called users) can thereby increase their profitability. This is a new form of inter-capitalist competition that will probably become more important in the years to come.

Or consider the case of mental agents contributing voluntarily to open-source (OS) projects through the Internet. Since they are not employed by capital, they are unproductive. They enjoy great freedom to apply their creativity. But the individual contributions might require coordination and thus a more or less formal organisation. This coordination can be the task of the project initiator or of those programmers with particular skills and commitment to the project. They decide which contributions to accept and give form and direction to the project. Wikipedia is a case in point.

The coordinators are often employed by IT firms. And thus they are productive.

---

14   Some mental producers can perform alternatively productive labour and the function of capital. See Carchedi, 1977.
15   See Carchedi, 2012: 220-225.
16   Ross (2013) is one of many holding this view.
17   For Kostakis (2012: 6) 'users produce value for firms.' For Reveley (2013) users are not producers of value. Users generate data passively and unconsciously (515), and are not 'primary producers' (516).
18   This is also what some blogs do. See Geert Lovink, Ossessioni collettive, Milan: Università Bocconi Editore, 2011: 22.

Who gains in this case? The knowledge so produced can either be appropriated by the firm 'lending' the coordinators or be free, in the sense that any other capitalist can appropriate it. In the former case, the advantage is obvious. By paying only one mental labourer (the coordinator), that firm appropriates the mental agents' collective knowledge and turns it into a source of profit.

But the firm can 'lend' a coordinator to a mental labour process without retaining the exclusive ownership of that knowledge. This apparent paradox is explained by a series of advantages accruing to the firms 'lending' mental labourers to this common project. First, the coordinator can accept only those contributions that fit that firm's techniques and interests. Second, that firm reckons that its advantages from such knowledge are greater than those accruing to its competitors. Third, by observing through the coordinator how the mental agents can be controlled and managed, that firm can draw useful indications as to how to control and manage its own mental labourers.

Some authors (Fuchs, 2010) deny that mental agents are unproductive and, following in the footsteps of workerism, extend the notion of exploitation beyond waged labour and into the whole of society. They argue that, since all labour is a condition for the reproduction of capital and thus for the production of surplus value, all labour is productive and capital exploits all members of society, non-stop. Two objections can be mentioned. First, to be the condition for the production of value is not the same as producing value. Collapsing the condition of production into actual production leads to absurd results. Since all labour is also a condition for the destruction of capital (crises, wars, etc.) all labour would also be destruction of capital. Second, if all labour is productive, why should capital try to increase the time that labourers work for it and reduce the labourers' free time?

Fuchs holds also that, given that Internet users (mental agents) are not paid for the production of value, the value of their labour power is nil. Thus, all the value produced by them should be regarded as surplus value that goes to capital. The rate of surplus value is thus infinite (Fuchs, 2010). But then, how can something that has no value (labour power) produce value and surplus value? And if all value were surplus value, the users *as* users would have to live on air.[19]

In reality, capital pays labourers for supplying labour for, say, eight hours per day. If the rate of exploitation is 100%, four hours are necessary to produce the wage goods (and thus to reconstitute the labour force for 24 hours) and 4 hours are surplus labour producing surplus product and thus surplus value. The reconstitution of labour power also implies recreation activities, including those on the Internet for, say, one hour a day. The same person who is a mental labourer for eight hours is a mental agent on the Internet for one hour, in her/his free time. Since in that hour that mental agent does not work for capital, s/he is not exploited and does not produce value and surplus value. The question of mental agents' rate of exploitation is thus meaningless. That mental producer is exploited not as a mental agent but as a mental labourer.

19   See also Henninger, 2007

The distinction between production and consumption

The third and final question concerns the *distinction between production and consumption* that the Internet is supposed to have made obsolete. This argument rests on a new figure, the so-called *prosumer*.[20] This term refers to mental agents whose production of knowledge co-determines the characteristics of an objective commodity that they commission through the Internet and then purchase and consume. The knowledge produced by that mental agent enters into and shapes the capitalist's objective production process, for example in the production of custom-made shoes. That mental agent participates in the design of the objective output: the shoes that this 'prosumer' subsequently purchases. However, it is one thing to argue that the same person is both a producer of a mental use value and consumer of an objective output; it is another to hold that the distinction between production and consumption has disappeared. Time is the key.

The knowledge produced by the mental agent is a mental use value that enters into and shapes the mental transformations determined by the capitalist's objective production process. The mental agent's consumption of the output of the capitalist's objective production process follows its production temporally. The present mental producer (mental agent) is the future consumer. The two phases are temporally distinct even if the same person might be a mental producer today and an objective consumer tomorrow. The prosumption thesis errs in that it cancels time. The prosumer is a figure of virtual reality, not of real reality.

The above is not to deny that 'users', i.e. mental agents, are the source of innovations in many fields (Lakhani & Wolf, 2005; Banks & Deuze, 2009; Prahalad &Ramaswamy, 2000). But behind the hype, the truth of the matter is that mental agents are a new source of productivity for corporations (Prahalad & Ramaswamy, 2000). An example of this is modding, the modification of video games by consumers (mental agents) using the tools provided by the manufacturers of the games. They are 'an increasingly important source of value for the games industry' (Küklich, 2005). The character behind the Janus face of the prosumer is not the empowered consumer but capital with new techniques to increase efficiency, sales, and profitability at no cost.[21] The idea that this new technology might replace mass production should be taken with a good dose of scepticism given that the future consumer brings only (marginal) modifications to mass produced commodities. 'In 2011 ... the Internet economy only contribute[d] 3.8% of the GDP of the EU27' (Pfeiffer, 2013:15).

Class knowledge and the Internet

The essence of capitalism is the contradiction between two fundamental classes: the owners and the non-owners of the means of production, and thus between the generators and the appropriators of surplus value. This contradiction also emerges at the level of cognition. The ownership of the means of production and thus the appropriation of surplus value require a view of reality that rationalises exploitation, inequality, and

---

20   See Rey, 2012, but also a host of other authors.
21   Or at the cost of its 'creative professionals', i.e. skilled mental labourers, inasmuch as the 'prosumers' replace them. See Banks and Deuze, 2009.

egoism. This is *capital's rationality*. Labour, to rid itself of capital's yoke, must express the opposite rationality. *Labour's rationality* must be based on co-operation, solidarity, and equality. The capitalists, to be such, must produce, or allow to be produced, a variety of views of reality whose common feature is that of being moulded by capital's rationality. The labourers, to resist capital's rule, must generate alternative views of reality with an opposite class content. Of course, there are more classes and many groups within them. But focus only on the two main classes is sufficient for the present purposes.

How can classes, aggregations of individuals who are by definition different, generate a knowledge shared by a number of individuals? How can social knowledge arise? The process of cognition involves two movements. They are contemporaneous but will be mentioned successively for the sake of exposition. The first movement is from classes to individuals.

For the system to reproduce itself, there must be individuals who rationalise its reproduction, no matter how. The capitalists, to be such, must rationalise, or allow to be rationalised, in a variety of ways, their own contribution to the production of wealth (value) in the form of profits. And there must also be individuals who rationalise, or allow to be rationalised, no matter how, resistance against the system and thus profits as the appropriation by the capitalists of a share of the value produced by labourers. The difference is that, as we shall see in a short while, mental labourers must work with the means of mental production owned by capital. Their resistance remains within the limits circumscribed by capital. Their cognition can transcend those limits only when they are free from capital's mental domination.

At this stage of the exposition, the specific features of these rationalisations are still undetermined. However, since classes are aggregations of individuals, these pro-capital and pro-labour rationalisations can exist and become manifest only in and through individuals, i.e. through specific, unique individual conceptualisations. Then, in principle, each individual internalises in his or her own way the rationality and interests of the class to which he or she belongs. But, through interaction with other individuals as carriers of other, opposite rationalities and interests, each individual can internalise different and opposite rationalities and interests. Thus, individuals give their own specific form to conflicting rationalities. Some of these cognitions can be consistent with, and some can be opposite to, the interests and rationality of the class to which an individual belongs objectively. The outcome is a kaleidoscope of depictions of reality, each with its own contradictory class content.

The class determination of knowledge holds at the aggregate, class, level because there must always be capitalists who conceptualise reality through the prism of capital's rationality and labourers who see the world through labour's rationality. But individual forms of knowledge are internally contradictory to the point at which a labourer's consciousness can either contain exclusively capital's rationality or be determined by that rationality. Who expresses one or the other rationality is a matter of chance. Social determination in one realm of reality (the system's need to express opposite types of rationality) manifests itself as a number of chance events in another realm of reality, that of concrete individuals and, vice versa, chance events in one realm of reality (that of the individuals) manifest themselves as social regularities in another realm (that of social classes). It is thus meaningless to seek a perfect match between a Weberian definition of class and individual class-consciousness.[22]

The second movement is from individuals back to classes. Individual forms of consciousness aggregate into views shared by a class. Since the elements of the aggregation are internally contradictory, and possibly mutually contradictory, the outcome of the aggregation is also contradictory. Moreover, given the internally contradictory nature of individual views, there are many aggregations that rationalise, each in its own way, the interests of a class. The process of cognition involves the clash of rationalities both between and within classes. These aggregations are not the simple summation of individual forms of consciousness because these specific manifestations are by definition different and thus cannot be added. There must be a common element that makes that aggregation possible. This is their shared class content irrespective of who shares it. This is why classes can reproduce themselves independently of which specific individuals, and thus which specific individual forms of consciousness, share that class content. There is no cognitive neutral space.

The aggregation of individual forms of knowledge requires the aggregation of mental producers who, following Gramsci, are here called organic intellectuals.[23] The organic intellectuals transform the variety of the specific individual forms of knowledge of the members of a group into their own view. Their representations become their individual, personal interpretation of a collective knowledge; they become the specific forms of a generality. The organic intellectuals and those they represent form the collective intellect of that group, the collective subjectivity, or knowledge, of that group.[24] Given the constant interaction between the organic intellectual and the other members of that group, the collective knowledge of that group is the product of the collective intellect and not only of the organic intellectuals. The organic intellectuals contribute and give a unified shape to that collective knowledge. Thus nothing could be further from the truth than that the collective subjectivity cancels individual identity.

Within a group there can emerge more than one organic intellectual. Each has a different interpretation of that group's knowledge and each view vies to become dominant. Also, within a group there might be sub-groups. Each can be represented by one or more organic intellectuals who operate at a lower level of aggregating capacity. Thus the collective intellect of a group can result from the interaction of the collective intellects of the several sub-groups. But this is not all. The organic intellectual of a group interacts with the general intellect and thus with the organic intellectuals of other groups. An organic intellectual can interiorise elements of a collective knowledge from a different class perspective until the original collective knowledge undergoes a radical change. The continuous struggle between these two rationalities to become dominant within each and all forms of knowledge is the cognitive class struggle: class struggle as production of knowledge.

22 Erik Olin Wright (1989) is the prominent sociologist who has worked with this methodology within a Marxist perspective. For a detailed critique, see Carchedi,1989.
23 Differently from Gramsci, here the organic intellectual aggregates the view and represents the interests of any social group.
24 This has nothing to do with the workerist notion of general intellect which generates knowledge through a mysterious, because never analysed, collective process of mental production.

As far as labour is concerned, this means that the defence and fostering of labour's rationality can assume different forms according to who becomes its intellectual representatives and that the capacity of its collective intellects to ward off capitals' rationality depends not only on the collective intellects' intellectual capacities but also, and mainly, on the interrelation between the multifarious forms of manifestation of all societal relations and processes both expressing and influencing the class struggle (e.g. the upwards or downwards long-term economic phase, the political power relations, the nature of labour's institutions and organisations from the smallest to the biggest, like the trade unions, etc.) and thus on the knowledge of the nature of that struggle.

If we apply the notion of the class content of knowledge to the analysis of the mental labour process (MLP) as above, the class content of knowledge as an output of an MLP is determined by the class content of the knowledge that goes into its generation. Then the analysis of how the social content of the knowledge as output derives from the social content of the knowledge as input implies the analysis of the social content of input. Since the input of one period is the output of the previous period, don't we fall into a backwards *ad infinitum* trap? No. The social content of knowledge as output can be determined independently of the social content of knowledge as input. But what if we want to understand how the input affects the output?

Let us choose a point of departure, for example time t1 as the end point of the period t0-t1. This period produces new knowledge, call it $K^N(t1)$.[25] At t1 we can analyse the social content of $K^N(t1)$ but not that of its mental input, the knowledge contained at t0 in labour power, i.e. $K^L(t0)$. The next production period, t1-t2, produces $K^N(t2)$. Its input is $K^N(t1)$, the output of the previous period, the social content of which is known. Since the output of a period becomes the input of the following period, $K^N(t1)$ as output of t0-t1 is at the same time $K^L(t1)$, the input of t2-t2. Then we can analyse how $K^L(t1)$ determines the social content of $K^N(t2)$. From t2 on, we can follow how the social contents of the mental inputs determine the social content of the newly generated knowledge.[26]

The thesis of the class determination of knowledge is rejected even by many Marxists, certainly when it comes to natural sciences. It is its use, it is held, and not its nature that is socially-determined, ie class-determined. Yet it is undeniable that, if the system must continue to exist in a contradictory way, there must be individuals who internalise class-determined cognitions. Then, their aggregations into shared cognitions, in other words the production of social knowledge, must be class-determined before that social knowledge can be used by one or the other class, or by both.

To clarify, let me consider two of the critics' favourite examples. First, a gun is supposed to be class neutral because both classes can use it. But a gun is the product of a society based on violence, in the last instance on the repression of labour by capital. Ultimately, it serves a class-determined need, the need of capital to continue to exploit

---

25 For the symbols KN, KL, and KO, refer back to relation (2) above. For the sake of simplicity, K0 is disregarded.
26 The same procedure allows us to answer the regression *ad infinitum* in the so-called transformation problem. See Carchedi, 2012.

labour and thus to reproduce itself. If a gun is used by labour, it serves the equally class-determined need of labour to resist exploitation. There is thus a *double* class determination, rather than no class determination. Its double class determination is inherent in its production because that production is the expression of a society divided between capital and labour. Thus the use of the gun by both classes is due to the gun's double class determination rather than it not being class determined.

The production of the gun determines the mental labour needed for that production. So if that objective production and its outcome are class determined, the mental labour they determine is also determined by capital's need to exploit labour. If the gun is used by labour to resist exploitation, the mental labour conceptualising that resistance is determined by labour's equally class-determined need to resist exploitation. An important conclusion follows: if knowledge is class determined, *all its constitutive elements are also class determined*. This conclusion is valid also for 2+2=4, another of the critics' favourite examples.

The critics hold that 2+2 is always equal to 4 in all societies and for all classes. Thus, 2+2=4 cannot be class determined. But first of all, 2+2 is *not* always equal to 4. It all depends on what we want to measure and on how we measure it. For example, our system of recording the time of the day goes from 0 to 24. Then, 23+1 is both = 24 and = 0 so that 24+2 is not 26 but 2. In mathematics, this is expressed as $26 \equiv 2$, *modulo* 24. Or consider clocks that use the numerals from 0 to 12. Then, 12 = 0 and $10+6 \equiv 4$, *modulo* 12, and not 16. Or consider a numerical system going from 0 to 4. Then $2+2 \equiv 0$, *modulo* 4. But once we choose a *modulo*, e.g. *modulo* 24, 2+2 is always equal to 4. What, then, can be said about its its social determination and content?

Primitive people did not conceptualise 2+2=4. They used expressions such as 'many people'. Numerical systems, and thus presumably 2+2 = 4, were determined by the emergence of exchange and commerce. As societies developed, the class determination of 2+2=4 changed. The need arose for different societies and different classes to measure and quantify irrespective of what is being measured and quantified. This need was and is common to contradictory rationalities. But this is not to say that it is not class determined. On the contrary, it is determined by more than one class because it is needed by more than one class to express forms of knowledge with a specific class determination and content. This I call 'multiple determination'. The specificity of multiple determination is that, in order to be consistent with opposite rationalities, it must be pure form without a visible class content. This holds for 2+2=4 as well as more generally for mathematics.

The critics perceive multiple determination, i.e. determination by more than one society or by more than one class, as lack of class determination. In so doing, they make a two-fold mistake. First, for them class determination implies necessarily the determination by only one class. They ignore multiple determination. Second, they fail to notice that if multiple determination abstracts from specific determinations, it does not erase them. They continue to exist potentially, hidden by multiple determination. This is why a specific determination, i.e. by only one class, can emerge again when that knowledge is immersed in a specific mental labour process. In other words, 2+2 =4 is determined by capital or by labour, and thus acquires its pro-capital or pro-labour class content, according to whether it is an element of a mental labour process informed basically by capital's or by labour's rationality. Far from not being class determined, 2+2=4 is at the same time determined both by more than one class (as a multiple determination, as a pure form) and specifically by only one class, when it becomes an element of a specific mental labour process.

The above has dealt with the production of knowledge in general under capitalism. Consider now MLPs carried out by mental labourers working for capital. They must transform existing knowledge into new knowledge with means of mental production owned by capital. What does this mean? The capitalists own the mental labourers' labour power. Consequently, the capitalists can decide which knowledge should be produced, how it should be produced, and for whom. Or, they have the power to define and solve problems (or let them be defined and solved) for their own goals, i.e. according to their own rationality. It is in this sense that they own the mental means of mental transformations which are also the means of mental production (KL in relation 2 above). It follows that the knowledge their mental labours produce must be informed either only by capital's rationality or also by labour's rationality. In the latter case, labour's rationality can become realised only within the contours of capital's rationality, and thus, only shaped and thus denatured by it.[27] As we shall see, labour's rationality can enter the production of this knowledge but only because it is denatured by capital's rationality. This is cognitive class struggle. Labour's false consciousness is not a distorted reflection of reality but the acceptance by labour of capital's rationality.

Usually, capitalists do not have the competence needed to organise and manage an MLP. This is the task of the collective intellect at their service. Within it, the organic intellectuals plan the structure of the MLP and formulate the tasks of the rest of the collective intellect and thus the structure of the MLP. This structure is fragmented in such a way that the collective intellect cannot reconstruct the overall view of the labour process. The structure of the production of knowledge by labour under capitalism is thus an instrument of labour's domination by capital. This is the hierarchical structure analysed first by Marx and in more recent times discussed in the Braverman debate. But there is also a different form of labour process, an MLP in which mental labourers are free to express their creativity subject to the ultimate approval and coordination of an agent of capital, for example a coordinator. The hierarchy is reduced to a minimum, but it is still there to ensure that these labourers produce surplus value. To this end, the organic intellectuals must have internalised the aims of capital and must have made them their own.

There is a feature specific to the production of knowledge under the rule of capital. In objective production, capital appropriates the product (and thus the value and surplus value contained in it) and nothing remains to labour. In mental production, capital owns the means of mental production and thus it appropriates the outcome of that process.[28] But that knowledge is also retained by the collective intellect. Capital appropriates the original, as it were, and the copy remains with labour. Then, the

---

27 The capitalists can pursue their own goals also indirectly, by defending the specific collective interests of those social groups in whose collective knowledge capital's rationality is dominant.
28 'The accumulation of knowledge and skill, of the general productive forces of the social brain [are] absorbed into capital.' Marx, 1973: 694.

collective intellect can use the copy of the knowledge it produces for its own purposes, and is thus also to resist the rule of capital.

However, capital's rationality predominates over labour's rationality because that knowledge has been produced by mental labourers with capital's means of mental production. Labour can use it to resist capital's rule but that resistance remains within the contours of capital's rule. For example, the rhythm of the assembly line can only be slowed down. Or, as we have seen, the use of a gun both by capital and by labour is not due to the class neutrality of the knowledge needed for its production but to its double class determination.[29] Labour can and must use it to resist capital's domination, but at the same time it acknowledges and accepts capital's rationality: the use of violence. Or take the knowledge needed for cooperation within a team of workers. The rules are not those that maximise the development of the workers' potentialities or the power to challenge capital's domination but those that increase productivity and thus profitability. Solidarity as viewed by labour has been transformed into a weapon of capitalist domination. Pharmaceutical firms do not produce those medicines that maximise human well-being but those that maximise profits.

Let us now come to the production of knowledge on the Internet. If it is produced by mental labourers, the analysis above applies. This explains the pro-capital knowledge inherent, for example, in video games.[30] If it is produced by mental agents, since it is not produced within the capitalist (mental production) relation, it can have a contradictory social content in which labour's rationality can (but does not necessarily) predominate. The generation of knowledge on the Internet is a battle for knowledge. It is part of the wider cognitive class struggle, between capital's and labour's rationality in its multifarious and ever-changing forms of manifestation. This knowledge, then, can be used to resist capital's rule. This is the real importance of the Internet.

The delusions of 'cognitive capitalism'

The apologetic analyses of the Internet are strictly connected to the notion of 'information society' and 'cognitive capitalism'. These are highly ideological concepts. The usual meaning of information is that it is communication of operational knowledge. In this view, information has no class content. This notion reflects and reproduces the myth of the class neutrality of knowledge. This is why in this essay I have used the term 'knowledge' rather than 'information'. The concept of cognitive society is equally ideological. As Henninger (2007) points out, the imagery of cognitive society is the way 'certain relatively privileged sectors of the world's working population' perceive contemporary capitalism. Even if, for the sake of argument, all objective labour processes were to disappear worldwide and only mental labourers were left, the old and debilitating features of capitalism would re-emerge, even if in a new guise. I consider only a few examples here.

---

29   This raises the issue of the role of non-violence in labour's strategy. This issue is beyond the scope of this article.

30   Dyer-Witheford and de Peute (2009) provide an excellent analysis of the ideological nature of virtual games. However, this study is embedded in a workerist frame, an approach radically different from that followed in this work.

On the Internet some mental labourers, e.g. some programmers in IT firms, can and must use their creativity to solve conceptual problems. This is a psychologically rewarding activity, often well paid. However, far from being a prefiguration of the working class of the future, they could be considered to be a new form of labour aristocracy. As such, in spite of their privileges, they are subjected to the rule of capital. They must apply their creativity (highly-skilled labour) also in their (mostly unpaid) free time. The skills they are under pressure to develop are those that can be used by capital, i.e. their conceptions are informed by capital's rationality. Their employment is subject to the ebb and flow of the economic cycle. As in objective labour processes, newly created highly-skilled positions are under constant threat of dequalification. A new form of proletarianisation emerges. The following passages are illuminating

Mechanical Turk is the innovation behind 'crowdworking', the low-wage virtual labor phenomenon that has reinvented piecework for the digital age. Created by Amazon in 2005, it remains one of the central platforms – markets, really – where crowd-based labor is bought and sold. As many as 500,000 'crowdworkers' power the Mechanical Turk machine, while millions more (no one knows how many exactly) fuel competitor sites like CrowdFlower, Clickworker, CloudCrowd and dozens of smaller ones. On any given day, at any given minute, these workers perform millions of tiny tasks for companies both vast (think Twitter) and humble. Though few of these people have any sense of their finished work product, what they're doing is helping to power the parts of the Internet that most of us take for granted.

As CrowdFlower's Biewald told an audience of young tech types in 2010, in a
moment of unchecked bluntness: 'Before the Internet, it would be really difficult to find someone, sit them down for ten minutes and get them to work for you, and then fire them after those ten minutes. But with technology, you can actually find them, pay them the tiny amount of money, and then get rid of them when you don't need them anymore.' (Marvit, 2014)

The rate of exploitation of crowdworers can be even higher than that in many objective production processes (whether they are aware of it or not). As Marvit (2014) says in discussing crowdwork, 'Since 2005, Amazon has helped create one of the most exploited workforces one has ever seen.'

The knowledge generated by mental agents can also be shaped by capitalist rationality. This is the case with projects that rest on the contribution of a number of mental agents. A large number of them aim at being hired by capital. The skills they develop must then be suited to the needs of capital. The freedom of their creativity and their much-touted 'playbour' is thus constrained. But, inasmuch as their mental production is not influenced by capital's rationality, they can generate a type of knowledge whose class content is alternative to that of capital. An example is provided by the thirteen-minute political documentary *The French Democracy* on the uprising by immigrant youth in 2005 in the suburbs of Paris. This video 'made for a cost of some $60, was downloaded many times, for free, was uploaded to YouTube, drew widespread press attention, and was shown at film festivals, making it perhaps the single most effective communiqué from the banlieues to leap across the Atlantic and around the world.' (Dyer-Witheford & de Peuter, 2009:187).

The case studies reviewed in this work have highlighted specific novelties. Those novelties are new bottles containing old wine: capitalism and its double, contradictory rationality. This thesis is further and definitely supported if we look at the wider picture. In the words of the *Economist*:

> The prosperity unleashed by the digital revolution has gone overwhelmingly to the owners of capital and the highest-skilled workers. Over the past three decades, labour's share of output has shrunk globally from 64% to 59%. Meanwhile, the share of income going to the top 1% in America has risen from around 9% in the 1970s to 22% today. Unemployment is at alarming levels in much of the rich world, and not just for cyclical reasons. In 2000, 65% of working-age Americans were in work; since then the proportion has fallen, during good years as well as bad, to the current level of 59%. (Economist, 2014).

This is exactly what Marx would have predicted. What the *Economist* forgets to mention is that in the last 30 years cognitive capitalism has been plagued by a series of crises, each worse than the one before. And, after 15 years of explosive growth of the Internet known as Web 2.0, the world economy has never been in such a bad shape since the 1929–33 crisis.

Contemporary sociological literature has generated a host of examples of how mental agents' interactions through the Internet and the forms of knowledge springing from these interactions, provide glimpses of a social structure based on labour's rationality as well as specific forms of resistance to capital's rule. But it would be a dangerous illusion to think that a simple multiplication of these attempts can lead to a radical societal change if the capitalist production relation is not thrown into the dustbin of history. The Internet does not cancel the divide between capital and labour and thus does not change the law of value. The theory of knowledge built upon the law of value rests on sound foundations. This theory can help us to understand how the Internet provides a global arena where specific form of knowledge arise, interact, and attempt to change each other, i.e. how the Internet reshapes the multitude of the cognitive forms of manifestation of the capital/labour contradiction. These forms of knowledge can be productive of value if produced under the rule of capitalism. To analyse them, one need not discard Marx's value theory. It is sufficient to apply it.

© *Guglielmo Carchedi, 2014*

REFERENCES

Arvidsson, A. & E. Colleoni (2012) 'Value in Informational Capitalism and on the Internet', *The Information Society*, 28 (3):135-150.
Banks, John A. & Mark Deuze (2009) 'Co-creative Labour', *International Journal of Cultural Studies*, 12(5): 419-431.
Carchedi, G. (1977) *On the Economic Identification of Social Classes*, London: Routledge and Kegan Paul.
Carchedi, G. (1984) 'The Logic of Prices As Values', *Economy and Society*, 1984 13 (4):431-455.
Carchedi, G. (1989) 'Classes and Class Analysis', in E.O.Wright, *The Debate on Classes*, London: Verso.
Carchedi, G. (2001) *For Another Europe. A Class Analysis of European Economic Integration*, London: Verso.

Carchedi, G. (2005) 'On the Production of Knowledge', *Research in Political Economy*, 22:267-304.
Carchedi, G. (2012) *Behind the Crisis*, Chicago: Haymarket.
Dean, J. (2010) *Blog Theory*, Cambridge: Polity.
Dyer-Witheford, N.& G. de Peuter, (2009) *Games of Empire*, Minneapolis: University of Minnesota Press.
Denton, P.H. & S. Restivo, (2008) *Battleground Science and Technology*, Westport, Conn.: Greenwood Press.
Economist (2014) 'Coming to an office near you', *Economist*, January 18, leader article, uncredited.
Henninger, M. (2007) 'Doing the Math: Reflections on the Alleged Obsolescence of the Law of Value under Post-Fordism', *Ephemera*, vol. 7(1):158-177.
Kostakis, V. (2010) 'Identifying and Understanding the Problems of Wikipedia's Peer Governance. The Case of Inclusionists versus Deletionists, *First Monday*, 15 (3).
Kostakis, V. (2012) 'The Political Economy of Information Production in the Social Web: Chances for Reflection on our Institutional Design', *Contemporary Social Science*, 7 (3):1-15. Accessed July 3, 2014, from http://p2plab.gr/wp-content/uploads/2013/05/CSS_Kostakis.pdf.
Küklich, J. (2005). 'Precarious Playbour: Modders and the Digital Games Industry', *The Fibreculture Journal*, 5.
Lakhani, K.R. & R.G. Wolf (2005) 'Why Hackers Do What They Do: Understanding Motivation and Effort in Free/Open Source Software Projects', in J. Feller, et al. (eds) *Perspectives on Free and Open Source Software*, Cambridge, Mass.: MIT Press.
Legault, M.-J. (2013) 'IT Firms' Working Time (De)regulation Model: a By-product of Risk Management Strategy and Project-based Work Management', *Work Organisation, Labour and Globalisation*, 7 (1):76-94.
Lovink, G. (2011) *Ossessioni Collettive*, Milan: Università Bocconi Editore.
Marvit, M.Z. (2014) 'How Crowdworkers Became the Ghosts in the Digital Machine', *The Nation*, February 4.
Marx, K. (1967) *Capital*, vol. III, New York: International Publishers.
Pfeiffer, S. (2013) 'Web, Value and Labour', *Work Organisation, Labour and Globalisation*, 7 (1): 12-30.
Pitts, F. (2013) 'A Science to it': Flexible Time and Flexible Subjectivity in the Digital Workplace', *Work Organisation, Labour and Globalisation*, 7 (1):95-105.
Prahalad, C.K. &V. Ramaswamy (2000) 'Co-opting Customer Competence', *Harvard Business Review*, January.
Rey, P.J. (2012) 'Alienation, Exploitation, and Social Media', *American Behavioral Scientist*, 56 (4): 399-420.
Reveley, J. (2013) The Exploitative Web: Misuses of Marx in Critical Social Media Studies, *Science & Society*, 77 (4):512-535.
Riehle, D. (2007) 'The Economic Motivation of Open Source Software: Stakeholder Perspectives', *Computer*, IEEE Computer Society, 40 (4):25-32.
Ross, D (2013) 'The Place of Free and Open Source Software in the Social Apparatus of Accumulation', *Science & Society*, 77 (2):202-226.
Starosta, G. (2012) 'Cognitive Commodities and the Value Form', *Science & Society*, 76 (3):365-392.
Stalder, F. (2013) *Digital Solidarity*, Post-Media Lab and Mute Books, Lüneburg: Leuphana University, accessed July3, 2014 from http://www.metamute.org/sites/www.metamute.org/files/u1/Digital-Solidarity-Felix-Stalder-9781906496920-web-fullbook.pdf.
Struik, D. (1948) 'Marx and Mathematics', *Science & Society*, 12 (1):181-196.
Terranova, T. (2000) 'Free labor: Producing Culture for the Digital Economy, *Social Text*, 18 (2): 63;33-57.
West, J. & S. Gallagher (2006) 'Challenges of Open Innovation: the Paradox of Firm Investment in Open-Source Software', *R&D Management*, 36 (3).
Wichita State University, Department of Mathematics and Statistics., Accessed July 3, 2014 from http://www.math.wichita.edu/history/topics/num-sys.html#mmmmm.
Wright, Erik Olin (ed.) (1989) *The Debate on Classes*, London: Verso.

Theories of immaterial labour:
a critical reflection based on Marx

Henrique Amorim

Henrique Amorim is Professor of Sociology in the Department of Social Sciences at the Federal University of São Paulo, Brazil.

ABSTRACT

Proponents of the notion of a 'knowledge economy' argue that immaterial labour is the main productive force in contemporary society. This article takes issue with this view. It critically assesses the concepts of labour, value and class that underlying these arguments and seeks to find alternatives to them. It then goes on to propose an alternative interpretation that, in the author's view, is more closely aligned to the general principles of Marxist theory. It concludes that the 'knowledge economy' theorists demonstrate an analytical reductionism: by limiting the definition of 'labour' to physical industrial labour performed in a factory, by reducing the concept of 'value' to an arithmetically measurable expression of exploitation in the manufacture of goods, and by restricting the concept of 'working class' or 'proletariat' to the position of the manual labourer. It concludes that the thesis which presents immaterial labour as a new productive force and announces the end of labour, value and the working class ignores the realities of the processes of labour precarisation currently taking place around the globe.

Introduction

Labour, value and class are fundamental concepts in Marxist[1] theory. Throughout his critique of political economy, Karl Marx consistently organises his analysis of capitalist society within a theoretical framework based on the interaction between three inter-related factors: the analysis of the exploitation of wage labour; value as the substance of this exploitation (to constitute surplus value and capitalist profit); and how these processes of exploitation and valorisation have historically divided society into classes.

The relationship between the concepts of labour, value and class is first synthesised

---

1   I highlight here the concepts of labour, value and class as the most fundamental concepts in Marx's work. However, they are of course closely linked with a large number of other concepts. A detailed discussion of these is beyond the scope of this article.

In Marx's work in *German Ideology* (2007 [1845-46]), gaining depth in many of his subsequent writings and reaching an essentially completed version in *Capital* (1998 [1867]). Sometimes emphasising conjunctural and political aspects, and at other times social and structural ones, Marx developed a theoretical framework in which the concepts of labour, value and class are mutually determined, taking into account the particular historical circumstances of Europe in the 19th century.

This context included the accelerated growth of industry, with the development of new productive forces (machinery) and huge masses of labourers, the chaotic expansion of cities, the rise of social and political conflicts associated with the need for productivity increases, labour intensification, long working hours, appalling working conditions and low wages. It also saw the emergence of labour organisations (socialist, communist and anarchist), including the Communist League, workers' conferences, revolutionary papers and journals. These were some of the historical features that shaped Marx's analysis of European capitalist societies and it was by generalising the historical and social processes that he witnessed that he delineated the essential contours of the relationship between capital and labour.

This conceptual tripod (of labour, value and class), which structures Marx's problematic, has had its validity questioned in recent decades. At the centre of this critique is the thesis that contemporary capitalist society has somehow moved its dynamic centre beyond production and factory labour. The argument is not that labour and the production of commodities has ended. Rather, it is asserted that commodity production is being replaced by new kinds of social activity that, together or separately, are bringing into being new forms of social organisation and politics (e.g. Inglehart, 1997; Offe, 1994; Bell, 1977; Touraine, 1970; Habermas, 1987).

This argument starts from the proposition that a Marxist approach can only be applied to an analysis of the forms of production that emerged in Europe at the beginning of the 18th century and culminated in the 1960s (e.g. Dahrendorf, 1982). This period encompassed the introduction of machinery and industrial development, and the continuing spread of this type of production throughout the 19th century, augmented by Taylorist rationalising management practices. In the early decades of the 20th Century, the technological apparatus of control and social domestication introduced by Henry Ford in the United States brought further developments. Such a perspective also assumes that, in the long period between the 18th century and the 1960s, production was based mainly on the manual labour of factory workers who also shared a common culture, habits, ideologies, feelings, social and party affiliations, due to the fact that they had more or less similar jobs. Because of their position at the centre of commodity production, these workers, seen as forming a homogenous mass, were assumed to be the main potential agents of the socialist revolution.

It is then argued that manufacturing industry lost its hegemony from the 1960s onwards, due to changes in the patterns of production, especially with the introduction of Toyotism[2], microelectronics and automated machinery. From then on, production was no longer characterised by the predominance of manual work that had prevailed

---

2   Toyotism is a term that refers to the kind of 'lean production' model developed at Toyota during the 1980s..

from the 18th century until the 1960s. Toyotist production did not seem to follow the previous pattern of production, and presented intellectualised labour as the new, and main, productive force in contemporary capitalist societies. The productive paradigm was seen as outdated, and, along with it, so was the idea of workers as an indistinguishably homogenous mass.

At first sight, the new 'flexible production' model, sometimes referred to as 'Toyotist', appeared to diverge significantly from its predecessor. With the introduction of industrial automation, the typically Fordist type of labour, which linked the labourer to a specific workstation as a machine operator, with work processes determined by the specific needs of the manufacturing method, became redundant. This was replaced by automated machinery and working processes that did not involve direct physical inputs. The worker was now 'left out of the working process in the strict sense' (e.g. Fausto, 1989), becoming a machine-minder rather than an operator: with no direct involvement in the working process itself, workers became mere 'keepers' of the machines. Furthermore, the surveillance activity which now constituted the main content of their work was no longer linked to a single machine, so they were expected to carry out several different tasks. The versatile worker, in this new industial environment, was responsible for the functioning and maintenance of a variety of different robotic machines, a responsibility that required intellectual qualifications, not just physical skills. This created the potential for conflict and divisions within the workforce. Just as the introduction of new technologies was making large numbers of manual workers redundant from the now-automated factories, the new production methods required the recruitment of new types of workers with intellectual skills and knowledge: that is, workers who had knowledge and information as constitutive elements of their professional qualifications.

In order to justify the supposed break with the production models that had prevailed up to the 1960s, the theorists of the 'knowledge economy'[3], saw no better way of making their point than to use Marx's own thesis. This enabled them to kill two birds with one stone: they could simultaneously both demonstrate the tendency towards the replacement of material by immaterial labour, and refute Marxist theory. It was in this context that Marx's *Grundrisse* (2002/2011 [1857-58]) was lavishly introduced into the discussion in order both to describe the shift from material to immaterial labour, as predicted by Mark himself in this work, and to demonstrate that this development was, in turn, the result of the automatic development of the productive forces of industry, i.e. it arose from within industry itself (Amorim, 2013).

Faced with this revolutionary perspective on the productive forces, and arguing that knowledge could not be the source of value because of its immensurability, the relation between working time and free time was presented by these thinkers as the key to understanding the stagnation of industrial production. In this view, since Marxism was supposedly a theory of industrialism, it had demonstrated its own obsolescence. Therefore, there would not be a revolution, but instead a transition; not

---

3   In this article I have grouped together several authors who hold the view that immaterial labor tends to be the primary productive force of capitalism in contemporary capitalist societies. Borrowing from Gorz, (2005) I have used the term 'knowledge economy' to characterise what is common in their approach. There are, of course, differences between these authors, who are cited separately where this is relevant.

a rupture, but a natural erosion; not a class struggle, but a rearrangement and political conciliation among heterogeneous groups.

Following this line of argument, free time becomes the measure of wealth, replacing necessary working time as a measure of value. The passage from Marx's *Grundrisse* that was most often used to support this proposition is the following:

> What capital adds is that it increases the surplus labour time of the mass by all the means of art and science, because its wealth consists directly in the appropriation of surplus labour time; since value is directly its purpose, not use value. It is thus, despite itself, instrumental in creating the means of social disposable time, in order to reduce labour time for the whole society to a diminishing minimum, and thus to free everyone's time for their own development. But its tendency is always, on the one side, to create disposable time, on the other, to convert it into surplus labour. If it succeeds too well at the first, then it suffers from surplus production, and then necessary labour is interrupted, because no surplus labour can be realized by capital. The more this contradiction develops, the more does it become evident that the growth of the forces of production can no longer be bound up with the appropriation of alien labour, but that the mass of workers must themselves appropriate their own surplus labour. (Marx, 2002: 639-640).

Taken out of its general context in Marx's broad oeuvre and its specific context in the *Grundrisse*, this excerpt suggests that the development of immaterial forms of labour (which could be termed 'cognitive') can be viewed as a social tendency which began in the most economically developed societies (Western Europe, USA and Japan) in the 1960s, and will inevitably extend to the periphery of capitalism. The growth of immaterial productive forces can thus be presented as the main tendency in the development of capitalism, a tendency which exposes the limits of the relationship between capital and labour.

This proposition marks the central question addressed in this article: what concepts of labour, value and class underlie the current arguments that immaterial labour is the main productive force in contemporary society?

In the early 1990s, Marício Lazzarato, Antonio Negri and André Gorz were among those who raised the issue of immaterial labour, developing specific interpretations of the concepts of 'labour', 'value' and 'class'. I describe their ideas as 'specific interpretations' because they cannot be evidenced in Marx's work, despite being related to concepts that are used in the broader spectrum of Marxist theory. In other words, although framed in Marxist terms, the thesis that immaterial labour is a central productive force builds its interpretation apart from Marx. The proponents of this approach produce a definition of 'labour' based on the manual (physical) labour that takes place in factories; they conceive 'value' as an arithmetically measurable expression of this manual labour and the 'working class' or 'proletariat' as a synonym for the class made up of these manual workers, which is the main agent of the valorisation process and, therefore, the revolutionary agent *par excellence*.

In the attempt to clarify differences between the concepts of labour, value and class as defined by Marx and the interpretation of these concepts within the framework of a 'knowledge economy', I aim here to introduce an alternative reading which takes as its starting point Marx's analysis of production processes, which are historically determined by social antagonism, and to analyse them using the concepts of labour, value and class found in Marx. In order to do so it is necessary to clarify the differences between material and immaterial labour as well as the relationship between immaterial labour, the production of surplus value and class. In addition, it is useful to identify evidence that can make it possible to locate the place of immaterial labour in the present historical conjuncture, characterised by the precarisation of working conditions.

Immaterial and material labour

How can we measure the conceptual differences between material and immaterial labour? In the works of Gorz (2005), Lazzarato (1992; 1993), Negri (2002; 2004) and Lazzarato and Negri (1991), immaterial labour is, essentially, labour with no physical substance. It is labour that is predominantly based on intellectual production, usually related to services, administration, management and control of the working process but also to some productive activities – those with labour processes that involve the use of knowledge and information. Viewed from this perspective, knowledge and information can be seen as the 'hard core' of immaterial labour.

This type of labour, according to Gorz (2005), in contrast with manual labour, stimulates creativity and prompts workers to think, take responsibility for decision-making and engage in other forms of intellectual activity. Cumulatively, this creates a 'knowledge economy' because these knowledge-based activities become '…the main source of value and profit, thus … the main form of labour' in contemporary societies (Gorz, 2005:29). However, such activities have a double dimension. Whilst these activities are considered to be the source of value, they are also revealed as immeasurable, because their fundamental component (knowledge) can no longer be reduced to an abstract amount of labour (Gorz, 2005:25). This gives immaterial and cognitive labour the peculiar characteristic that it is seen as the *result* of the intellectual content that is inscribed within it. Following this logic, Gorz constructs immaterial labour as the opposite of manual labour, with the latter seen as a functionally homogenous kind of labour completely lacking any cognitive dimension.

Lazzarato (1990), in turn, basing his analysis on a study of the technological changes implemented in Toyotist factories in the 1960s and 1970s, argues that the tendency is towards a replacement of specialised workers by versatile workers. These versatile workers, in his view, will develop a new kind of subjectivity, a subjectivity of 'commanding', quite different from the subjectivity produced under Taylor-Fordism before the arrival of automation and robots. The versatile worker's job is not standardised, making it progressively more difficult to measure his or her activity because it is 'built over decisions increasingly more difficult to be prescribed' (Lazzarato, 1990:158). According to Lazzarato, the immediate consequence of this is that in the capitalist organisation of production, capital, dependent as it is on their intellectual growth to generate profit, is forced to give their subjectivity back to the workers.

Combining elements from both Gorz and Lazzarato, Negri defines immaterial labour as that 'which produces immaterial commodities such as information, knowledge, ideas, images, relationships and affections' (Negri, 2004: 44), and that '… nowadays, in a period in which immaterial labour is predominant and generalised in terms of quality, the intellectual is found within the productive process [being, therefore] the new subject, constitutive power and potency of communism'. (Lazzarato & Negri, 2003).

In order to comprehend the relationship between manual and intellectual labour, it is also necessary to investigate the concepts of materiality in general and material labour in particular, to understand to what extent such concepts are not *ideal types* in dichotomous opposition to each other. To Marx, these concepts are concrete abstractions which are mutually determined; that is, they are concepts that express contradictory historical interconnections. These interconnections have specific characteristics, being shaped by the organisation of the activities involved in the elaboration and execution of production, which are manipulated by capital in many ways, with distinct contents in different social arrangements and historical conjunctures. Nevertheless, they have the shared aim of (re)organising the working class and reproducing its socially exploited and dominated class condition.

Such an analysis brings into question how intellectual labour can assume a position that is the polar opposite of manual labour. The answer is clear: it cannot! All human activity, whether under capitalism or other production forms, depends to some degree on intellectual labour. In the *Economic and Philosophic Manuscripts* (2004 [1844]), Marx observed that all human activity is a process of externalisation and, in his *Theses on Feuerbach* (1993, [1845]) he elaborated this argument that all human activity is a process of objectification of human subjectivity, that is, of putting oneself in the world, in a repeated, historically-determined synthesis, theoretically fracturing any methodological duality between subject and object. Here, Marx makes clear his position that any intellectual or manual human activity is based on the process by which subjectivity is made objective, a process in which a way of life is also produced. It is an objectification that has historical subjectivity as its fundamental mark. Thus, manual and intellectual labour are concepts that express a contradictory reality. In terms of an analytical process of conceptual determinations, they allow a dialectical analysis of living labour, which is done by taking into account the predominance of manual or intellectual activities depending on the way that they appear.

Intellectual and manual labour are not independent of this historical process of successive objectification. They are in fact the expression of these objectifications. They can, however, be differentiated sociologically. Within a Marxist framework, these differences can be related to variations in the content of labour. There are, for example, groups of workers who dig, who mine, who plant, who operate machinery, who produce electronic gadgets, who manage the processes of labour, who assemble, who design machines and nuclear bombs, and so on. These differences relating to the content of the labour are complicating factors in the technical organisation of these groups, in education and training policies and in investment in private industry, which, taken together, (re)organise the means of increasing labour productivity with the aim of maximising capitalist profit.

For its own utility, capital encourages a proliferation of professional qualifications. And these differentiated activities can be understood as the basis for a concept of *concrete labour*, a concept that recognises that each form of labour has its own characteristics and is distinguishable from others. It is not Marxist theory but actual social development that has established labour markets in which these singularities are dissolved. The intrinsic character of labour *as labour*, however, is not constituted by any of these particularities but by common characteristics. Marx called this common element, which is present in all labour in capitalist society, *abstract labour*, defining this as the average working time socially necessary for the production of commodities. Commodities are not exchanged for their use values, but for the value of the labour that is crystallised in them. Thus, concrete labour, which is particular, specific and distinguishable, is subordinated, historically and socially, to abstract labour; that is, to a general labour that expresses different values, which makes it socially interchangeable.

Abstract labour is, therefore, presented by Marx in *Capital* (1998) as a regulator of market exchange. Hence the singularities of concrete labour are not important in themselves; they are simply the means by which it is possible to increase the productivity of abstract labour in order to valorise capital. In this sense, capitalist entrepreneurship is not focused on particular sectors but invests in the production of a range of different commodities: sometimes, for instance, book production, at other times car production, music (Vinyl/CD) production or software production; sometimes generating the need for manual labour and at other times for intellectual labour, and most of the time combining all these forms of labour unequally. Each investment is considered purely in terms of its possibilities for generating profits based on the exploitation of working hours, an exploitation that varies in intensity according to the labour legislation of the country in which it is located.

Contrasting with this, the central arguments put forward by Gorz (2005), Negri (1992), Lazzarato (1993) and Moulier-Boutang (2007) in the debate about the immateriality of labour are attached to the content of labour; that is, to the concept of concrete labour. They project the development (inside capitalism), firstly, of professional qualifications that are not subordinated to capital and, secondly, of social subjects who will exacerbate the insubordination of immaterial labour, due to its singular and revolutionary character.

This conclusion comes from a vulgar notion of wage labour which detaches the production of intangible commodities from the forms of production that are typically capitalist. To these authors, the immateriality of labour is not determined by the means of production but by the content that is created or manipulated in the processes of this labour. Thus, the proponents of the idea of a 'knowledge economy' come to the conclusion that the brutality and roughness of manual labour sit in opposition to the creativity, intelligence and versatility of immaterial (cognitive and intellectual) labour as if these two forms were separated by radically different objective conditions. Such arguments are completely contrary to those of Marx, who reminds us that:

> A commodity is, in the first place, an object outside us, a thing that by its properties satisfies human wants of some sort or another. The nature of such wants, whether, for instance, they spring from the stomach or from fancy, makes no difference. (Marx, 1998:45)

Hence the production of knowledge or automobiles may or may not be under conditions historically predetermined by capital. Production is not determined by the content of the labour and the products that derive from it. What is highlighted here is the means by which this production was organised, regardless whether it is of tangible or intangible commodities. If the intention is to produce the largest number of products in the shortest possible time using wage labour, this inevitably entails the production of surplus value.

Finally, the dominance of immaterial labour proclaimed by the 'knowledge economy' theorists, suggests that the production of industrial commodities, and hence the Marxist theory that explains it, is defunct. Extrapolating from the reduction in the number of factory-based jobs in Europe, Japan, and USA since the 1960s and the rise of immaterial labour, they forecast that the economy based on the production of value will fade out of existence. The materiality of labour is confused with its physical nature. This interpretation entails an analytical reductionism, in the sense that it regards only the elements of production as solid, but not the social relations, the values, the symbolic expression and political confrontations resulting from class struggle, which structure this production.

Immaterial labour and labour value

When developing the general argument presented in this article, my first intention was to demonstrate that the concepts of labour, value and class held by proponents of the 'knowledge economy' hypothesis are based on a reductionist misconception of Marx and to expose the fundamental features of the historical materiality of capitalist production, emphasising the mutual determination between the concepts of manual labour and intellectual labour. However this discussion gives rise to a further dialectical unfolding, in the sense that a discussion of the production of value raises the question: what are the types of production and labour that produce value? To the knowledge economy theorists, this can only be the forms of production that are based on manual labour and measured by the time spent in carrying out this labour.

It is therefore necessary to go beyond the arguments in the previous section of this article and dig more deeply into the social relations of contemporary capitalism in order to make explicit the mistaken arguments that, according to Moulier-Boutang (2007), underlie the 'cognitive capitalism' thesis. In particular, there is a need to explore what the aforementioned authors mean when they refer to the production of value, and to compare their understanding of the term with Marx's definition of value. This is because their conception of value is critical to their thesis that capitalist societies are now tending towards a new type of social organisation (called 'cognitive capitalism') which they present as an alternative to the critique of capitalist political economy and the need to overcome class antagonism based on the contradictory relationship between capital and waged labour.

Some aspects of this hypothesis can be refuted empirically. For instance, it is noticeable that the number of workers employed in ITC-related occupations has increased substantially in the last decade.[4] The majority of these jobs are carried out for

---

[4] In Brazil, for instance, according to data from the Annual Relation of Social Information (RAIS) and the Ministry of Labour and Employment (MTE), the number of employed telemarketing operators more than tripled, from 125,000 to 419,000 workstations, between 2002 and 2013. In the same period the number of computer system analysts increased from 89,000 to 250,000 workstations.

large capitalist companies which employ this labour force on precarious contracts with poor working conditions and high rates of staff turnover. In relation to their scope for creativity or control over their labour processes, there is little or no difference between these workers and Fordist workers. Telemarketing operators in Brazil, for example, express high rates of dissatisfaction with their working conditions and have elevated rates of occupational illness, attributed to the repetitive and routine nature of their work, heavy supervision and rigid control rules, related to the imposition of tight productivity targets, leading to high rates of drop out.

Returning to Marx, in order to clarify this aspect of the debate, we can ask to what extent value can be arithmetically calculated or measured. This question is addressed in the 'knowledge economy' literature on the assumption that the value of labour can be determined as an arithmetically measurable element. But, in *Capital*, Marx does not take this approach. He identifies value as the result of 'a productive expenditure of human brains, nerves, and muscles' (Marx 1995-96:26), which becomes a commodity when its direct utility is denied and which can be exchanged for other commodities in the form of an abstract quantity of labour.

In contrast, the 'knowledge economy' approach claims to see in the *Grundrisse* elements that justify the argument that capitalism will be overcome through immaterial production. Gorz, for instance, says that labour 'is no longer time-based. The factors which determine the concept of value **[become]** the behavioural and motivational components, not the time spent' (Gorz, 2005:10). He adds that when knowledge becomes capitalised a new situation is created, a situation in which human and physical effort is no longer required for its circulation. 'The more it is disseminated, the more useful it is to society; on the other hand, the more it is disseminated, the less market value it has, tending to zero.' (Gorz, 2005: 10).[5] This brings into being a 'knowledge economy' in which market relations and capitalist exchange have been overcome. This conception of immaterial production problematises the production of value in the sense that it makes it impossible to quantify the value produced in immaterial commodities using time measures. Such an economy is thus the negation of capitalism.

This quotation from the *Grundrisse* is often drawn on to support this argument:

> (...) To the degree that large industry develops, the creation of real wealth comes to depend less on labour time and on the amount of labour employed than on the power of the agencies set in motion during labour time, whose 'powerful effectiveness' is itself in turn out of all proportion to the direct labour time spent on their production, but depends rather on the general state of science and on the progress of technology, or the application of this science to production. (The development of this science, especially natural science, and all others with the latter, is itself in turn related to the development of material production). (Marx, 2002:636)

Marx was here developing a kind of abstract logical exercise, speculating about what would happen if dead labour were to replace living labour completely (by the

---

5   In *Les Chemins du Paradis*, Gorz says: 'Working time can no longer be the measure of economic value. The salary must not be depend on the amount of work, nor the right to an income be subordinated by the pursuit of employment' (Gorz, 1983:69).

development of science and technology applied to production) and taking this to its logical conclusion.[6] At first sight, this passage would seem to imply a logical, ahistorical, transformation, resulting from the development of capitalism itself and not based on class struggle. But if we consider the whole picture it is doubtful that Marx would attribute to the development of the productive forces the role of transforming social relations or confer the status of autonomy onto these relations. This is clear from his statements elsewhere, for instance where he states that that:

Wealth is not command over surplus labour time (real wealth), but rather, disposable time outside that needed in direct production, for every individual and the whole society' (Marx, 2002: 638).

On the one hand, Marx envisages working time being reduced by science and technology; on the other, he understands wealth as the available time used for production across the entire society.

These two quotations represent two sides of the same coin. When projecting the development of the capitalist forces, Marx understands that the material conditions for the structural transformation of capitalist societies are already present within themselves. In other words, he does not offer Utopian edification on the need for the political construction of socialism, but argues that the elements which allow such revolutionary construction evolve from capitalism itself. However (on the other side of the coin), he also alerts us to the fact that, based only on capitalist productive development, there is no possibility that revolutionary entrepreneurship can be achieved, since it is not materially possible that 'each individual and the whole of society' can enjoy the time available. This refers to the assumption, always present in Marx, that the appropriation of commodity production in capitalism and, thus its available time, is always private.

Capitalist society, therefore, is orientated to achieve more and more productive surplus, but the time 'released' in the process by which living labour is transformed into dead labour does not emerge in the form of freedom, but in the form of unemployment, outsourcing, third party contracts, intensification of labour exploitation and drastic reductions in labour security, indirect wages and social rights. In capitalist societies (except in mass hysteria) the time released by scientific development and the technologies applied to commodity production is not made available to the working class, since this time is released in a negative way. A reduction in necessary working time (material or immaterial) does not automatically result in making the extra time available for all society, because the release of time is directed towards reducing labour costs, lowering the cost of commodity production and thus increasing the rate of surplus value taken privately by capital. Capitalist production is still based, as it has always been, on shedding labour wherever possible and intensifying the exploitation of those workers who have managed to keep their jobs.

---

6   It is exactly from this deterministic interpretation of the productive forces (science and technology applied to production) that Gorz draws his understanding of the historical process when he states that: '[Technological progress] leads ... inevitably to the question of the content and meaning of available time. Moreover: [it is necessary to] question the nature of a civilization and a society that value the increase of available time [over] the increase of working time and for which, consequently, economic rationality does not rule over the time of all' (Gorz 1988:17-18).

Why not invert the question and understand this process of using the intellectual workforce as one more development through which capital advances in order to increase its own value? Why not analyse this process as a continuation of the forms of exploitation which, over the last 40 years, have linked the production of information- and communication-based commodities to the production of clothes, shoes, automobiles and houses? Finally, why should the intangibility of immaterial commodities prevent the generation of value from their production?

As we attempt to demonstrate in this section, the answer given by the 'knowledge economy' apologists to the last question is based on a misunderstanding of the concept of the value of labour, especially the notion of working time used by Marx. In the belief that only the production of physical commodities is counted by capital as producing value, immaterial production is seen as the negation of capital because it cannot be quantified in time units. Hence, instead of examining how capitalist society is itself produced, the 'knowledge economy' proponents focus on how production is organised within capitalism; and instead of looking at the social relations within which immaterial production takes place, they highlight the physical or abstract substance of the raw material used for such production. Materiality is then understood as a synonym for palpability. Thus the historical perspective based on the synthesis of conflicting social relations is reduced to the materiality of physical things, as if these things were not also an expression and synthesis of social relations.

Immaterial labour and class

We have reached one of the most controversial issues in the discussion of immaterial labour: the relationship between the immateriality of labour and forms of political struggle. If manual labour and labour value have supposedly been made obsolete in an economy founded on knowledge and information, the logical deduction of the authors who support this line of thinking is that the subjects of this process, the working class, must fall as well.

According to the 'knowledge economy' proponents, the working class prevailed politically for three centuries up until the1960s. This working class was made up of workers carrying out repetitive manual work, rigidly controlled by supervisors and foremen, in which the functions and productive specialisations were predominantly homogenous and easily controlled by capital, and linked to a specific form of factory production. From the 1960s onwards, this homogenous class was replaced by a heterogenous range of political subjects, brought into being by the transformation of production, leading to an automated and flexible form of industrial organisation.

Although containing an enormous variety of occupations and wages, and also strongly differentiated by ethnicity, colour, gender, geographical, political and ideological diversity, according to these theorists, the workers of the Taylor-Fordist industries, throughout the world, were united by the homogeneity of their productive activities. Sharing the fact that their labour involves the transformation of physical raw material into commodities, these workers could be considered throughout the 20th century as synonymous with the working class or proletariat, a class centrally defined by its place in the production process.

It is from this definition of the working class that the 'knowledge economy' proponents present their thesis. In their view, the workers of the new economy can no longer be seen as a class because the range of their occupations, activities, professional qualifications, skills and knowledge has become so broad that they are now too diverse to be defined as part of the working class which, in their view, is constituted by homogeneity of labour processes, skills and work content. It follows from this that if the production of tangible commodities in factories is declining and the production of intangible ones is increasing, we can no longer analyse capitalist societies using Marx's concept of class. If what defines class is nothing more than its social and occupational elements, than the Marxist concept of class has become outdated.

It is worth going back to *Capital*, most specifically to Chapter 52, entitled 'The Classes', (Marx, 1998: 297-298), to see how Marx himself uses the concept of class. This makes it possible to revisit the debate on the role of classes in immaterial production and qualify the way that these concepts have been appropriated in contemporary debates.

Although unfinished, Chapter 52 provides clear evidence that Marx went beyond a purely economic approach to class. He starts by describing how the capitalist social structure apparently presents itself, based on three classes: capitalists, wage workers and landowners. These three large social groups are based on common identities defined in relation to their income: wages, profits and rents.

Starting from this apparent form of representation of individuals in social groups, Marx then subdivides these social groups based on their position in the production process and the income they receive from their occupations. In this initial moment, Marx defines social class only in terms of socioeconomic determinations. In practice, the capitalist, working and landowning classes are social strata. Unfolding Marx's way of thinking we can characterise these classes using social criteria other than income and work position in the production process. For instance we could classify them in relation to criteria such as status, merit, professional qualification (whether manual or cognitive), race, age, prestige, number of electronic products in the family residence or the frequency with which they go to the movies, football matches or the opera.

However, as the following quotation shows, deepening his thoughts, Marx suggests that if we limit ourselves to the surface of the socio-economic determination of income and functional distribution we have to admit that:

> (...) physicians and officials, e.g., would also constitute two classes, for they belong to two distinct social groups, the members of each of these groups receiving their revenue from one and the same source. The same would also be true of the infinite fragmentation of interest and rank into which the division of social labour splits labourers as well as capitalists and landlords – the latter, e.g., into owners of vineyards, farm owners, owners of forests, mine owners and owners of fisheries. (Marx, 1996: 610)

As Marx points out, if we were to follow this logic we would have as many classes as there are professional and qualification-based subdivisions and, related to these, income subdivisions. That is, the concept of class would be completely diluted and would become indistinguishable from social notions of category and professional occupation, based on theories of social stratification.

Nevertheless, an idea developed in mainstream 20th century Marxism that social classes and, in particular, the working class could be defined only by the income and position that individuals hold in the production process, a notion that Marx himself had already criticised in the 19th century, as already noted. For instance, Nikolai Bukharin in *'Historical Materialism: a system of Sociology'* (n.d. [1921]) defines class as '(…) a group of people playing the same role in production (…). From this, based on the process of product division, each class is unified by the identity of their source of income. (…)' (Bukharin, n.d:323). This interpretation of class prevailed among the Marxist theorists influenced by the Communist Party during the 20th century. Theirs is an interpretation that absolutely coincides with the one which Marx criticised, an interpretation that he demonstrated to be circumscribed by superficial social appearances, based on social stratification criteria (e.g. **Gramsci, 2004; Poulantzas, 1977; Thompson, 1998).**

Strictly speaking, there is no direct causal relationship between occupational identity, whether material or immaterial, and political class unity. Firstly, if this causal relationship is assumed, social class is reduced to the specific features of particular working processes; and secondly, it promotes a determinist derivation in which a group of workers can project themselves as a social class based only on the fact that they do the same jobs and have similar incomes. So when the 'knowledge economy' theorists propose that class divisions will be overcome by a supposed heterogeneity of function, income and professional qualification, they should direct their criticisms at the reductionist Marxist concepts developed by Communist Parties during the 20th century. Based on this reductionism, which was bolstered by a mechanistic distinction between what were deemed to be 'productive' and 'unproductive' forms of labour and workers (Amorim, 2009; 2013), the task of identifying the workers who make up the working class was simplified. Productive workers were taken to be the historical agents of the socialist revolution and social class transformation. In addition to this, the notion of the working class or proletariat was conceived in a positivist fashion as made up only of a countable set of individuals employed in similar occupations.[7]

This contraposition of a professionally heterogeneous group to a homogenous working class, in order to demonstrate the decay of the latter, represents a major difference from the type of analysis adopted by Marx himself. In the political conjuncture analysis he developed, for instance in *The Class Struggles in France* (2012) and *The Eighteenth Brumaire of Louis Napoleon* (2011), a much more sophisticated approach is adopted, in which political, ideological and economic dimensions are correlated to qualify the configuration of social classes in specific historical contexts. None of these elements, whether economic or not, takes precedence when Marx observes the configuration of French social classes and the relationship between these classes from 1848 to 1850.

In short, when the 'knowledge economy' proponents posit the working class as opposed to immaterial workers, the former is considered to be a homogenous mass defined only according to workers' position in the production process and their income. This is in fact a contraposition of two professional categories, not of two social classes:

---

7   Bensaïd refers to this issue, showing how the French Communist Party ideologically used a restrictive concept of the working class to determine which workers could become revolutionary political subjects (Amorim, 2010).

one category that is based on manual work and another based on intellectual work. In this conception, the working class is defined based on a supposed homogeneity that does not consider patterns formed by ideology and political culture, or of domination and values. This analytical reduction restricts the definition only to determinations of income, function or professional qualification and does not provide any means to understand the emergence of a new (working) class, whether at Ford in Michigan in the 1930s or Foxconn in Shenzhen in 2010.

The exploitation of labour in the contemporary world

When considering to what extent the use of the workforce in contemporary societies combines the exploitation of labour that is predominantly manual and that which is predominantly intellectual, it is useful to make a distinction between 'industry' and 'the factory', a distinction which seems to have been ignored in debates about the 'knowledge economy'.

It is in their failure to differentiate between these two concepts that the 'knowledge economy' proponents have encountered the difficulties that have led to their failure to recognise the exploitation of intellectual workers that prevails in typical capitalist production. In assuming that Marx's theory only applies to industrialism, the thesis on which this perspective is built takes 'industry' and 'factory' as synonyms and, observing the reduction in the number of jobs in factories manufacturing durable goods, concludes that this type of production will be replaced by immaterial production.

However, contemporary capitalist industry, although still growing in its traditional forms, has been restructured and takes new forms that connect the typical Fordist production model, in which a large group of labourers work in the same place under a rigid regime of work, to new forms of labour that are organised in networks, direct or indirect, linked to large companies that sell their products at very low cost. Labour exploitation has been exacerbated by the incorporation of new forms of labour without defined working times, but based on targets (that is, the incorporation of managerial responsibilities by collective labour), together with third-party contracts and subcontracts, and labour forms taking place outside the scope of formal contracts, such as slave labour.

We are witnessing not the extinction of the capitalist mode of production, but, on the contrary, its deepening and strengthening. Hence the concept of industry cannot be reduced to that of the factory. Capitalist industry determines a type of organisation based on the production of commodities and the exploitation of labour for profit. Whenever this type of production is imposed, other forms are necessarily subordinated to it, reproducing this type of production.

What Ricardo Antunes (2013) has called the 'new morphology of labour' partially sums up this idea. Throughout the world, there has been a vertiginous growth in industries and services linked to telecommunications, and jobs related to these technologies have grown along with them. In Brazil, for example, this development was linked to the privatisation of Brazilian public companies, initiated under the presidency of Collor de Mello and radically deepened by the Fernando Henrique Cardoso government. Assuring a flow of rent from this expanding sector enabled capital to cross a new productive boundary during this period. This allowed the private productive apparatus to build profitable new forms of immaterial production, with the help of the state.

Strengthened by Toyotist forms of work organisation and management, employment in ICT-based services in Brazil has expanded over this period and this has been accompanied by increased stress, hypertension and high staff turnover rates, developments that are particularly evident in telemarketing companies. Rosso (2008) is one of several researchers who have drawn attention to the way in which immaterial labour has been associated with growing work intensity and workload, creating a situation in which workers' health has been put at risk. As previous issues of *Work Organisation, Labour and Globalisation* have shown, such scenarios can also be found in the USA, Europe and China. In such a situation, how is it possible to argue that wage labour, the value of capital and the working class have been abolished? Or even to speculate that contemporary societies are not determined by the production of commodities which articulate wage labour, the production of value and the necessary presence of the working class in this process?

Contrary to the 'knowledge economy' thesis, industrial production in Brazil and in the rest of the world continues to be grounded in the production of commodities. According to the World Bank (2011), industrial production of durable goods in the gross domestic product of India rose from 20% to 28% between 1960 and 2008. In China this ratio increased from 37% to 47% in the same period. The number of workers in Brazil employed in telecommunications production or services increased from 1,665,000 to 2,438,000 between1994 and 2011 (Teleco/Telebrasil, 2011; CAGED, 2011).

Conclusion

From the arguments presented above, it can be concluded that capital aims to combine the production of material and immaterial commodities, in the process articulating distinct regions, technologies and managerial approaches. The combination of traditional industrial production with newer forms, drawing on cognitive labour, has broadened capital's domination and exploitation of labour, resulting in the extreme subordination of the working class. The thesis which presents immaterial labour as a new productive force and announces the end of labour, value and the working class is based on a perspective which ends up supporting the central precepts of the current process of labour precarisation.

© Henrique Amorim, 2014

REFERENCES

Amorim, H. (2009)*Trabalho imaterial: Marx e o debate contemporâneo*, São Paulo: Editora Annablume.
Amorim, H. (2013) 'O tempo de trabalho: uma chave analítica'. *Sociedade e Estado* 28 (3):503-518.
Amorim, H. & L. Galastri (2010) 'Teoria do valor, trabalho e classes sociais: entrevista com Daniel Bensaïd', *Revista Crítica Marxista* 30:93-102.
Antunes, R. (2013) 'A Nova morfologia do trabalho e suas principais tendências', R. Antunes (ed), *Riqueza e Miséria do Trabalho no Brasil II*, São Paulo: Boitempo:13-27.
Bell, D. (1977) *O Advento da sociedade pós-industrial: uma tentativa de previsão social*. São Paulo: Editora Cultrix.
Bukharin, N. (1970) *Tratado de materialismo histórico*, Lisboa: Centro do Livro Brasileiro.

CAGED (2011). Accessed on June 12th, 2011 from: https://granulito.mte.gov.br/portalcaged/paginas/home/home.xhtml
Dahrendorf, R. (1982 [1957]) *As classes e seus conflitos na sociedade industrial*, Brasília: Ed. Universidade de Brasília.
Fausto, R. (1989) 'A Pós-grande indústria nos *Grundrisse* (e para além deles)'. *Lua Nova* 19:47-67.
Gorz, A. (1983) *Les Chemins du Paradis: L'Agonie du Capital*, Paris: Galilée.
Gorz, A. (1987) *Adeus ao Proletariado - Para Além do Socialismo*, Rio de Janeiro: Editora Forense.
Gorz, A. (1988) *Métamorphoses du Travail. Quête du Sens: critique de la raison economique*, Paris: Galilée.
Gorz, A. (2005) *O Imaterial: conhecimento, valor e capital*, São Paulo: Editora Annablume.
Gramsci, A. (2004) *Cadernos do Cárcere*, Rio de Janeiro: Civilização Brasileira.
Habermas, J. (1987) *Teoría de la Acción Comunicativa*, Madrid: Taurus.
Lane, J. F. (2011) 'Disaffection in the Post-Fordist Workplace: Figurations of "Immaterial Labour" in Recent French Theory and Literature', *Modern & Contemporary France* 19 (4):495–509.
Lazzarato, M. (1990) 'Les caprices du flux – les mutations technologiques du point de vue de ceux qui les vivent', *Futur Antérieur* 04:156-165.
Lazzarato, M. (1992) 'Le concept de travail immatériel: la grande entreprise'. *Futur Antérieur* 10:54-61.
Lazzarato, M. (1993), 'Le cycle de la production immatériel', *Futur Antérieur* 16, 1993:111-120.
Lazzarato, M. & A. Negri (1991) 'Travail Immatériel et Subjectivité', *Futur Antérieur* 6:87-99.
Marx, K. (1968) 'Matériaux pour l'économie (Théories de la plus-value), 1861-1865. In: *Oeuvres*, Paris: Gallimard/La Pleiade, tome II.
Marx, K. (1974) *O 18 Brumário e Cartas a Kugelmann*, Rio de Janeiro: Editora Paz e Terra.
Marx, K. (1993) *Teses sobre Feuerbach*, São Paulo: Editora Hucitec.
Marx, K. (1998) *O Capital*, São Paulo: Editora Nova Cultural.
Marx, K. (2002), *Elementos Fundamentales para la Crítica de la Economia Política (Grundrisse/Borrador)*, Buenos Aires: Siglo Veintiuno Argentina Editores.
Marx, K. (2004) *Manuscritos econômico-filosóficos*, São Paulo: Boitempo Editorial.
Marx, K. (2011) *Grundrisse: Manuscritos Econômicos de 1857-58: esboços da crítica da economia política*, São Paulo: Boitempo Editorial.
Marx, K. (2012) *As Lutas de Classe na França*, São Paulo: Boitempo Editorial.
Marx, K. & F. Engels (2005) *A Ideologia Alemã*, São Paulo: Boitempo Editorial.
Moulier-Boutang, Y. (2007) *Le Capitalisme Cognitif: La nouvelle grande transformation*, Paris: Éditons Amsterdam.
Negri, A. (2002) 'O empresário político', A. Urani et al (eds), *Empresários e empregos nos novos territórios produtivos: o caso da Terceira Itália*, Rio de Janeiro: DP&A.
Negri, A. (2003) 'Capitalisme cognitif et fin de l'économie politique'. *Multitudes* 13: 197-205
Negri, A. (2004) 'De l'Avenir de la Democracie (Débat avec Olivier Mongin)', *Alternatives Internationales* 18:44-47.
Offe, C. (1989) 'Trabalho: a categoria-chave da Sociologia?', *Revista Brasileira de Ciências Sociais* 10 (4):06-20.
Poulantzas, N. (1977) *Poder Político e Classes Sociais*, São Paulo: Editora Martins Fontes.
RAIS (2011) Accessed on June 12th, 2011 from: http://www.rais.gov.br/
Rosso, S. D. (2008) *Mais Trabalho! A intensificação do labor na sociedade contemporânea*, São Paulo: Boitempo Editorial.
Telebrasil (2011) Accessed on June 12th, 2011 from: http://www.telebrasil.org.br/panorama-do-setor/consulta-a-base-de-dados.
Teleco (2011) Accessed on June 12th, 2011 from: http://www.teleco.com.br/.
Thompson, E. P. (1998) 'Algumas observações sobre classe e 'falsa consciência''', S. Silva & A. Luigi (eds) *A Peculiaridade dos Ingleses e Outros Artigos* (*Textos Didáticos*, n. 10).
Touraine, A. (1970) *Sociedade Pós-Industrial*, Lisboa: Moraes Editores.

ACKNOWLEDGEMENTS

An earlier version of this text was published in Portuguese in *Caderno CRH*, 27 (70), 2014.

Review: From Silicon Valley to Shenzen: global production and work in the IT Industry

Enda Brophy

Enda Brophy is an Assistant Professor in the School of Communication at Simon Fraser University in Vancouver, Canada

Book reviewed
Boy Lüthje, Stefanie Hürtgen, Peter Pawliki and Martina Sproll (2013) From Silicon Valley to Shenzen: Global Production and Work in the IT Industry. Rowman & Littlefield. ISBN: 9780742555884, hardcover, 276 pages.

In June 2010, Foxconn workers in Guadalajara, Mexico staged a solidarity vigil for their colleagues half a world away. In China, a series of suicides had highlighted the dismal conditions of work and life at the world's largest and most notorious contract electronics manufacturer, rapidly becoming a public relations disaster for Apple, the world's most valuable brand. The suicides and the vigil pointed to the inescapably material conditions of possibility for capitalism's growing communicative requirements – most importantly the emergence of a sizeable transnational and industrial working class needed to manufacture the information technology hardware. Both the tremendous expansion of markets for consumer gadgets and the informatisation of industries across the broader economy have, in recent decades, been premised on the parallel rise of this workforce and the electronics industry it toils within.

The development, crises and successive transformations of this industry, in all of their regional specificities and complex dynamics, are the focus of this important book by Boy Lüthje, Stefanie Hürtgen, Peter Pawliki and Martina Sproll. Compressed within its pages are the findings of a collaborative research project conducted from the Frankfurt Institute of Social Research between 2001 and 2010. The result is a comprehensive overview, by authors with ties to the labour movement, of a quintessentially transnational industry, the trajectory of which invites us to rethink theories of global political economy and the labour process.

Translated from its 2009 appearance in German, the text has the great merit of offering not only a study of electronics mass production from the restructuring and expansion of the American IT sector in the 1980s and 1990s until the period immediately following the global financial crisis of 2008, but also a valuable account of the manner in which the development of electronics production has unfolded within, across and between the key global regions of 'low-cost' manufacturing. As if this were not sufficient, the authors seek to go further by revealing the manner in which the global production strategies adopted by electronics companies play out on the shop floor for the vast, mostly female and typically migrant workforce assembling the world's gadgets. The result is a study of notable ambition, tracing the globalising dynamics of post-Fordist electronics production and (although, as we shall see, to a lesser extent) the parallel composition of a 'neo-Taylorist' factory-based workforce.

The recent history of the electronics industry is narrated through two stages the authors associate with the regions named in the book's title – Silicon Valley and Shenzen. In the first stage, under the 'Wintelist' system that emerged in the 1990s in the PC industry, dominant brand-name players became 'companies without factories of their own' (9) as most production was outsourced to external contract manufacturers according to what is described as the electronic manufacturing services (EMS) model. In this first remaking of the industry, propelled by finance capital, US-based contract manufacturers 'took over entire chains of production, supply and logistics for complex products such as PCs, laptop computers, and cell phones' (10). Brand-name companies limited themselves to designing the technology, thus extricating themselves from the harsh realities of factory production in a classic example of post-Fordist outsourcing.

The period investigated by the authors has been a deeply unstable one however, both for the electronics industry and the wider economy. The book does a particularly good job of connecting the restructuring of the electronics sector to the major economic crises that have disrupted economic production since the 1990s. The period after the crucially formative dotcom bust of 2001-2002, for example, saw the decline of the Wintelist model and the emergence of a new breed of global subcontractors that began to take over the remaining factories of well-known electronics companies such as IBM, Lucent, Siemens, and Ericsson. Building gargantuan production sites in Mexico, Eastern Europe, Malaysia, and, above all, China, these contract manufacturers employed thousands of workers and extended the capacity of electronics brands such as Apple to engage in what the Los Angeles Times aptly called 'stealth manufacturing'. The destructive creation of the dotcom crisis spurred a competing model of electronics production, described in the industry as original design manufacture (ODM) and featuring the increased integration of product development itself within the manufacturing services offered by third-party firms. This new production model, as noted by the authors, further 'hollows out' the productive and innovative resources of global electronics firms – almost all that remains is the brand. Crucially, this development also creates a new round of competitors for brand-name companies like Apple. In the period following the 2008 crisis, Asian firms such as Acer, Lenovo and Huawei emerged as contenders in electronics production.

Conceptualising the shift in the centre of gravity of global electronics production 'from Silicon Valley to Shenzen' is useful for understanding the developmental dynamics of this industry, but cannot fully transmit the complex 'economic, social and political multipolarity of the process' (217). Drawing on political economy and industrial sociology, the authors seek to position the wealth of empirical data produced out of their project within a theoretical framework that can explain the development of this industry and the 'world-market factories' within which its profits are made (184).

Older models of the globalisation of production, above all that of the New International Division of Labour (NIDL), are no longer adequate to this task, the authors propose, suggesting instead a shift toward understanding the restructuring of electronics manufacturing as 'network-based' mass production. Network-based mass production, as the authors note, is a 'strategy to cope with the structural problems of post-Fordist capitalism caused by the overaccumulation of capital and industrial overcapacity' (219). Marked by a 'dialectics of decentralisation and recentralisation of capital' which constitute its 'basic dynamics' (219), such production has determined 'various types of large-scale industrial clusters ... in a small number of low-cost locations, each with specific dynamics of clustering or de facto integration' (224).

The approach adopted by the authors in this book will not be for everyone. A sizeable chunk of the detail provided, for example, will only be of interest to specialists. The narrative style is austere. In what could be described as a political economy from above, the analytical perspective taken by these authors privileges capital almost exclusively, making it seem for long stretches as if it is the only actor on the stage – with the vast workforce it depends upon described almost as an afterthought. Accounts of the labour process have very little of the richness provided by inquiries carried out in collaboration with workers and their associations, and foregrounding their stories, that have been offered by scholars such as Lisa Sun-Hee Park and David Pellow in *Silicon Valley of Dreams* (2002), or, more recently, in Jack Qiu's *Working Class Network Society* (2009). Most disappointingly, the book concludes by dismissing the subjective capacity of global electronics workers to make a difference in changing the barbaric conditions marking their work, proposing the 'institutionalisation of enforceable legal and contractual standards' (238) instead. How these standards might be forced upon the companies in the electronics industry in the absence of widespread and sustained worker' struggles and organising is altogether unclear – especially given the evidence the authors present. The book makes mention of instances of rebellion and collective organisation by workers, many of them significant, but again these are presented only as a kind of addendum to the strategies and dynamics of capital in the sector.

These are, in the end, only minor objections, however. The authors have succeeded in producing a tremendously well-documented and useful account of the development of global electronics capital. This book stands as an authoritative overview of this history and makes a contribution that will be of great value to critical scholars in a range of fields.

© Enda Brophy, 2014

Review: Flip-flop: a journey through globalization's backroads[1]

Liz Heron

Liz Heron is an independent writer based in London, UK.

Book reviewed
Caroline Knowles (2014) Flip-Flop: A Journey Through Globalization's Backroads, Pluto Press.ISBN: 9780745334110, paperback, 232 pages.

I've known Caroline Knowles for a number of years and from time to time I've heard accounts of her research trips to Africa, Asia and elsewhere. Once I emailed her and got a reply from a rubbish tip outside Addis Ababa where she was busy with interviewees. She doesn't stick to the safest, most comfortable routes on a trail, and she is more intrepid than her university will allow her to be.

The trail she's been following is the life cycle of the flip-flop, and the results have recently been published. In *Flip-Flop: a Journey through Globalisation's Backroads* she tracks the manufacture of the flip-flop, from the plastic's liquid source in the Kuwaiti oilfields to the petrochemical factories of South Korea, where polyethylene and other thermoplastic resins are made, to be shipped onwards to China and the flip-flop factories around the city of Fuzhou. China has ten major container ports from which some fifteen million tons of manufactured goods are transported annually worldwide. From their forty-odd destinations Caroline chose Ethiopia as her endpoint; it's a significant importer of flip-flops and now also produces its own (and has even started making shoes for export to Italy). That huge rubbish tip outside Addis Ababa is where the worn out articles end their days, there to be rescued (and sold for recycling) by large numbers of scavengers – modern-day *chiffoniers* who depend on their pickings for a livelihood, risking injury as they vie with the bulldozers.

Whether it's the scale of Chinese shipping, the economic background to piracy in the Gulf of Aden, the chemistry of plastics or the mechanised processes of production, Caroline is punctilious in mapping the global traces of this lowly and low-cost product. The flip-flop does have its variations in quality and styling and can even be a pricey designer purchase, while at the same time being distinguished as the first form of footwear for many of the world's poor who hitherto went barefoot. Her book offers many insights into the chain of connections required for it to reach African market stalls and European or US department stores.

The book's real heart, however, lies in its probing of what all this means for the lives

---

[1] This review was first published on Liz Heron's blog at: http://lizheron.wordpress.com/2014/07/08/flip-flop/

of those engaged in such a globally connected enterprise, and some of those for whom these connections intersect with patterns of migration – although, as we all know from daily news reports, the movement of products and the capital inherent in them is much less constrained than that of individual workers desperate to escape poverty.

There are interviews with oil workers, from a geologist to managers and derrick men at a drilling operation in the desert north of Kuwait City. In South Korea, where migrants arrive from many other parts of Asia, there's an overview of the petrochemical boom. We learn about low-level entrepreneurship in China, about the gender division of labour in Chinese flip-flop factories, and the high-intensity demands made on some of these workers for rewards that fall far short of adequate living standards. In the Fuzhou Economic and Technical Development Zone (the Zones have their own rules and regulations) work is often precarious as rural migrants compete with the more settled labour force in and around the city. One couple interviewed, in their 80s, struggle to make a living after being torn away from farmland designated for industrial development.

People tell their stories of how work is organised and within what hierarchies, what pay means in terms of hugely varying living conditions and welfare provision, what potential exists for children's education and for secure old age. All these are explored and set within a context of everyday life and both social and physical landscapes. This focus shows us how globalisation is experienced at the local level and at the level of individual biographies.

The flip-flop trail is only one strand in the vast economic web that we know as globalisation. It's a good place to begin unpacking that term, to glimpse what the world's disparities in wealth and well-being might really mean. I'd recommend starting the trail with chapter two; the first chapter is really for sociologists curious about methodologies, and can more easily be read once you finish the rest of this brave and ambitious book.

©*Liz Heron 2014*

Lightning Source UK Ltd.
Milton Keynes UK
UKOW04f1945080914

238249UK00001B/13/P